Easy German

Fiona Chandler, Katie Daynes
and Nicole Irving

Designed by Katarina Dragoslavić
Illustrated by Ann Johns

Edited by Jane Chisholm
Series designer: Russell Punter

Language consultant: Florian Becker
Additional material: Sam Taplin

Cover designed by Zoe Wray
Cover illustration by Christyan Fox

Contents

About this book

This book provides an easy introduction to the German language. Each grammar page explains a particular topic, from nouns through to conditional sentences, with examples to show how German is used in everyday situations. The boxes shown below highlight different learning points, and there are recommended Web sites to give you further opportunity to put your German to the test.

This *Vorsicht!* box means "Watch out!" It warns you of mistakes you might easily make, and points out some of the differences between German and English grammar.

! Vorsicht!

The *Learning tips* box tells you more about German grammar patterns and gives you clues to help you learn them more easily.

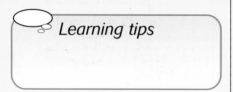

Learning tips

Each *Fast Facts* box contains an extra gem of information. Impress your friends with your detailed knowledge of German!

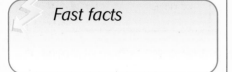

Fast facts

When new verbs and tenses are introduced, they are clearly presented in a verb box, with the English translation alongside.

Tun (to do)

▯ Internet links

Look out for the little computer symbol in the right-hand corner of each grammar page. Here you'll find descriptions of useful Web sites where there are quizzes, games and tests to practise your German. To visit the recommended Web sites, go to the Usborne Quicklinks Web site at **www.usborne-quicklinks.com** and type in the key words "easy german".

The recommended Web sites have been selected by Usborne editors as suitable, in their opinion, for children, although no guarantees can be given and Usborne Publishing is not responsible for the accuracy or suitability of the information on any Web site other than its own. Before using the Internet, please read the Internet safety guidelines in Usborne Quicklinks. You can find more information about Usborne Internet links on pages 124-125 of this book.

The Blumenkohl treasure: introduction

Throughout this book you can follow a story about a search for hidden treasure, using examples of the German grammar you'll be learning along the way. As new words crop up, they will be listed in the *New words* box. If you need extra help, there are translations of the speech bubbles on pages 100-111.

The main characters

Erich Müller

Tanja's brother. Likes walking, climbing, cycling and eating.

Tanja Müller

Erich's sister. One year older than him. Likes reading crime novels.

Monika Blumenkohl

Erich and Tanja's friend. Met them whilst on holiday last year.

Heidrun Blumenkohl

Monika's mother. A well-known sculptress. Runs the house on a tiny budget.

Franz Blumenkohl

Monika's father. Son of Georg Blumenkohl. Works for a charity.

Stefan Speck

A well-travelled crook. On file at Berlin police headquarters.

Der Kommissar

The local policeman. Doesn't take the three friends seriously at first.

Hüpfer

The Blumenkohls' dog. Tireless and brave, if a bit excitable at times.

Sometimes you will see this picture at the bottom of a page. It means there is a puzzle that needs to be solved. Look at the clues and try to figure out what Erich, Tanja and Monika should do next.

Understanding grammar words

Grammar is the set of rules that summarizes how a language works. It is easier to learn German if you know a few grammar words. All the words you use when you speak or write can be split up into different types.

A **noun** is a word for a thing, an animal or a person, such as "box", "idea", "invention", "cat", "woman". A noun is plural when you are talking about more than one, for example "boxes", "ideas" or "women".

cat

A **pronoun**, such as "he", "you", "me", "yours", is a word that stands in for a noun. If you say "The goat ate your clothes" and then, "He ate yours", you can see how "he" stands in for "goat" and "yours" stands in for "your clothes".

Is this **yours**?

An **adjective** is a word that describes something or someone, for example "blue", as in "a blue jacket".

blue

Prepositions are link words such as "to", "at", "for", "near" and "under", as in "she is under the water".

under the sea

A **verb** is an action word, such as "make", "play" or "eat". Verbs can change depending on who is doing the action, for example "I make" or "he makes". If you change a verb in this way, you **conjugate** it. Verbs have different **tenses** according to when the action takes place, for example "I make" or "I made". The infinitive form of the verb is its basic form: "to make", "to play" or "to eat". Dictionaries normally list verbs in this form.

to **play** football

An **adverb** is a word that gives extra information about an action. Many adverbs describe the action of a verb, for example "badly", as in "He plays tennis badly". Other adverbs describe when or where an action happens, for example "yesterday", or "here".

He plays **badly**.

Subject or object?

When used in a sentence, a noun or pronoun can have different parts to play. It is the **subject** when it is doing the action, for example "the dog" in "the dog barks", or "he" in "he barks". It is the **direct object** when it has the action done to it. For example, in the phrase "he brushes the dog", the dog is the direct object.

In the sentence "She gives money to the man", "she" is the subject, and "money" and "the man" are objects. "Money" is the direct object because it is the object that is being given. "The man" is the **indirect object** because the money is being given to him.

What are cases?

In German, nouns and pronouns change a little depending on what part they play in a sentence. For instance, their last letters may change. These different forms are called **cases**. The subject, direct object and indirect object all have different cases.

What is a clause?

A **clause** is a section of a sentence that has a subject and a verb. The main clause in a sentence is one that can stand alone. In the sentence "He shouted at the dog which was barking because it had seen a cat", the main clause is "He shouted at the dog". There are two other clauses: "which was barking" and "because it had seen a cat".

Laura passes the salad to David.
subject + verb + direct object + indirect object

Sarah drinks quietly.
subject + verb + adverb

Harry is bored.
subject + verb + adjective

Nouns

All German nouns are either masculine [m], feminine [f] or neuter [n]. These are called genders. The word for "the" shows the gender of a noun.

Saying "the"

- The masculine word for "the" is *der*.
- The feminine word for "the" is *die*.
- The neuter word for "the" is *das*.
- The plural word for "the" is *die* for all nouns, whatever their gender.

Masculine, feminine or neuter?

For some nouns, the gender is obvious:

e.g. *der Mann* (man) is masculine.

e.g. *die Frau* (woman) is feminine.

For most nouns, the gender seems random:

das Kino   *der Berg*
(cinema)   (mountain)

Some nouns have two forms:

die Freundin   *der Freund*   (friend)

Saying "a"

- The masculine word for "a" is *ein*.
- The feminine word for "a" is *eine*.
- The neuter word for "a" is *ein*.

Here are some examples:

ein Flughafen [m]   *eine Straße* [f]
(airport)   (road)

ein Hotel [n]   *ein Haus* [n]
(hotel)   (house)

8

Making plurals

In the plural, most German nouns add one or two letters at the end, and many also add an umlaut (¨):

der Mann (man) - *die Männer*
der Bahnhof (station) - *die Bahnhöfe*

die Frau (woman) - *die Frauen*
die Stadt (town) - *die Städte*

das Schloss (castle) - *die Schlösser*
das Kino (cinema) - *die Kinos*

Learning tips

• Try to learn nouns with *der*, *die* or *das* in front of them, so that you remember their gender.

• In dictionaries and word lists, nouns are usually written like this: *der Turm(-¨e)*. The letters in brackets are for making the plural, so you would learn this noun as: *der Turm, die Türme*.

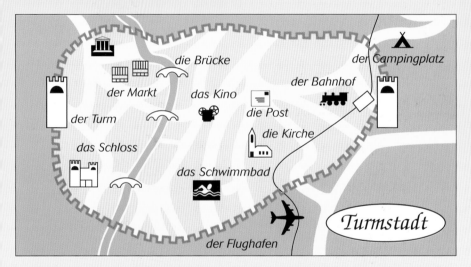

der Campingplatz
die Brücke
der Markt
der Bahnhof
das Kino
der Turm
die Post
das Schloss
die Kirche
das Schwimmbad
der Flughafen
Turmstadt

Vorsicht! (Watch out!)

• German nouns always start with a capital letter.

• The gender of some nouns is completely different from what you might expect. For example, *das Mädchen* (girl) is neuter!

• When making a noun plural, you usually add the umlaut above the last "a", "o" or "u" of the word. If the noun has an "a" and a "u" one after the other, you add the umlaut above the "a":

das Haus (house) - *die Häuser*

• When you add an umlaut to a plural noun, it changes the sound of the word. (See pages 98 and 99 for a guide to German pronunciation.)

9

The Blumenkohl treasure: chapter 1

Erich and his sister Tanja are flying to Turmstadt from Munich to spend a short holiday with their friend Monika Blumenkohl...

New words

der Berg(-e)	mountain
das Bonbon(-s)	sweet
die Brücke(-n)	bridge
das Dorf(-¨er)	village
der Flughafen(-¨)	airport
der Fluss(-¨e)	river
der Hafen(-¨)	port
das Haus(-¨er)	house
die Karte(-n)	map
die Küste(-n)	coast
der See(-n)	lake
die Stadt(-¨e)	town
der Turm(-¨e)	tower
auch	too, also
da ist/sind	there is/are
das ist	that is, it's
die beiden	both, the two
dort drüben	over there
es ist	it is
hier	here
ja	yes
schau, schau mal	look
toll	great
und	and
was ist das?	what is that?

As Erich and Tanja look at the map on their way in to land, the man sitting behind them is also studying it closely. He is working out the way to the Blumenkohl house.

11

Adjectives

In German, when an adjective comes before a noun, it changes. It has different letters added on the end, depending on whether the noun is masculine, feminine, neuter or plural.

Adjective endings

After *ein/eine*, you add **er** for masculine nouns, **e** for feminine nouns and **es** for neuter nouns.

ein grüner Koffer
(a green suitcase)

eine schwarze Tasche
(a black bag)

ein gelbes Zelt
(a yellow tent)

For plural nouns, add **e**, whether the noun is masculine, feminine or neuter, e.g. *blaue Hüte* (blue hats).

ideale Ferien (perfect holidays)

More adjective endings

After *der/die/das*, you just need to add **e** for all genders:

der rote Koffer (the red suitcase)
die große Stadt (the big town)
das kleine Dorf (the small village)

After *die* in the plural, add **en**:

die grauen Taschen
(the grey bags)

Sometimes, an adjective comes before a noun without using a word like "a" or "the". Then you add **er** for masculine nouns, **e** for feminine nouns, **es** for neuter nouns and **e** for plural nouns:

blauer Himmel (blue sky)
klare Luft (clear air)
rotes Gepäck (red luggage)
große Bäume (tall trees)

gute Reise! (have a good journey!)

grünes Gras (green grass)

ein schnelles Auto (a fast car)

When used after a noun, an adjective doesn't change, e.g. *das Auto ist schnell* (the car is fast).

First verbs

Verbs - or "action" words - change depending on who is doing the action. Many German verbs follow the same basic pattern, but some verbs have their own unique pattern. They are called irregular verbs and they need to be learned separately. Before the verb, you put either a subject noun (the dog, Peter, Mum, etc.) or a subject pronoun (I, you, he, etc.). This tells you who is doing the action.

I, you, he, she, etc.

I - *ich*

you - *du, ihr* or *Sie*
• Use *du* when talking to a friend or relative, or someone who is your own age or younger.
• Use *ihr* when talking to a group of friends, relatives or people your own age or younger.
• Use *Sie* when talking to an older person or someone you don't know very well. You also use *Sie* if you are talking to more than one older person or a group of people you don't know very well.

he - *er*
she - *sie*
it - *er, sie* or *es*
• There are three different words for "it". Use *er* for masculine [m] nouns, *sie* for feminine [f] nouns, and *es* for neuter [n] nouns.

we - *wir*

they - *sie*

Eine kleine Insel (A little island)

Two useful irregular verbs

Haben (to have)

ich habe	I have
du hast	you have
er/sie/es hat	he/she/it has
wir haben	we have
ihr habt	you have
sie haben	they have
Sie haben	you have

Sein (to be)

ich bin	I am
du bist	you are
er/sie/es ist	he/she/it is
wir sind	we are
ihr seid	you are
sie sind	they are
Sie sind	you are

Learning tip

Try learning verbs by saying them out loud. Practise writing them down too. Then cover up the German and test yourself!

blaues Meer (blue sea)

grüne Bäume (green trees)

schwarze Felsen (black rocks)

The Blumenkohl treasure: chapter 2

Erich and Tanja have landed at the airport, but there seems to be some confusion in the baggage claim area. There's a real scrum at the carousel...

Hallo, Monika? Hier spricht Tanja.

Wir sind in Turmstadt...

Danke, Sie sind sehr nett.

New words

der Ausgang(-¨e)	exit
das Gepäck	luggage
der Koffer(-)	suitcase
der Rucksack(-¨e)	rucksack
die Tasche(-n)	bag, pocket
das Zelt(-e)	tent
aber	but
blau	blue
danke	thank you, thanks
dein/deine[1]	your
Entschuldigung	excuse me, sorry
es geht	it's all right
Fräulein	Miss
grau	grey
groß	big, tall
grün	green
hallo	hello, hi
hier spricht	it's (here speaks)
Ihr/Ihre[1]	your (polite)
klein	small, short
mein/meine[1]	my
müde	tired
nein	no
nett	nice, kind
rot	red
schwarz	black
sehr	very
sein/seine[1]	his

[1]For more information about this kind of adjective, go to page 21.

Nein, es geht. Wir haben deine Karte.

Das ist deine Tasche.

Aber nein, das ist seine Tasche.

Mein Rucksack ist rot.

Mein Gepäck ist grau.

Hier ist Ihr Koffer, Fräulein.

Ausgang

Making the present tense

The present tense is used to describe what you do, or are doing, now. There are two main groups of verbs in German, known as "weak" verbs and "strong" verbs. In the present tense, both groups follow a very similar pattern.

Weak verbs

All weak verbs follow the same pattern. You take the infinitive of the verb (e.g. *machen*), remove the *-en*, leaving the stem *mach-*, and add the present tense endings:

Machen (to do)

ich mach**e**	I do/am doing
du mach**st**	you do
er/sie/es mach**t**	he/she/it does
wir mach**en**	we do
ihr mach**t**	you do
sie mach**en**	they do
Sie mach**en**	you do

Here are some more weak verbs that follow the same pattern:

besichtigen	to go and see
besuchen	to visit
kaufen	to buy
kochen	to cook
spielen	to play
suchen	to look for
tanzen	to dance

 Vorsicht!

German doesn't distinguish between the two forms of the English present tense: "I do" and "I am doing". So *ich mache* can mean either. This is the same for all verbs in the present tense.

Strong verbs

In the present tense, strong verbs use the same endings as weak verbs. But many of them have a vowel change with *du* and with *er/sie/es*. You need to learn these as you come across them.

Sehen (to see)

ich seh**e**	I see
du s**ie**h**st**	you see
er/sie/es s**ie**h**t**	he/she/it sees
wir seh**en**	we see
ihr seh**t**	you see
sie seh**en**	they see
Sie seh**en**	you see

Here are some more strong verbs that have a vowel change:

essen (er *isst*)	to eat
fahren (er *fährt*)	to go, to drive
geben (er *gibt*)	to give
helfen (er *hilft*)	to help
lesen (er *liest*)	to read
schlafen (er *schläft*)	to sleep

 Learning tips

• Learn the verb endings separately, then you can add them to any verb.

• In the word lists in this book, strong verbs will be marked by an asterisk (*). There is a list of strong verbs on pages 114-115.

What do you want?

The German for "to want" is *wollen*. *Wollen* is an irregular verb, so you have to learn it separately.

Wollen (to want)	
ich will	I want/am wanting
du willst	you want
er/sie/es will	he/she/it wants
wir wollen	we want
ihr wollt	you want
sie wollen	they want
Sie wollen	you want

I want to...

You can use *wollen* with another verb to say what you want to do. The second verb stays in the infinitive and goes to the end of the sentence, e.g. *Ich **will** das Schloss sehen*. (I want to see the castle.)

The nominative case

A noun is in the **nominative** case when it is the **subject** of a sentence (i.e. the person or thing that is doing the action). In the sentence "cows eat grass", the noun "cows" is the subject. In the word lists in this book, nouns are given in the nominative case.

The accusative case

A noun is in the **accusative** case when it is the **direct object** of a sentence (i.e. the person or thing that the action is being done to). In the sentence "I kick the ball", the noun "ball" is the direct object.

In the accusative case, the words for "the" and "a" change if the noun is masculine singular. *Der* changes to *den*, and *ein* changes to *einen*. The adjective ending is -*en*, e.g. *Ich will ein**en** groß**en** Orangensaft*. (I want a large orange juice.)

Ich will das Schloss besichtigen.
I want to go and see the castle.

Entschuldigung, ich suche den Bahnhof.
Excuse me, I'm looking for the station.

Ich will eine Cola.
I want a coke.

Ich suche ein Hotel.
I'm looking for a hotel.

Und ich will die Kirche sehen.
And I want to see the church.

Okay. Dort drüben ist ein Café.
OK. There's a café over there.

Ich will nach Hause fahren.
I want to go home.

The Blumenkohl treasure: chapter 3

Erich and Tanja have managed to collect their bags from the airport and are now on their way to Monika's house. They stop at a café for a rest...

A man walking past Tanja dropped a letter. By the time she picked it up for him, he had driven away.

Oh!

Wir wollen Fahrräder leihen.

When she looked, the letter was very strange. It was written to a son called Georg and signed Tobias Blumenkohl...

Eine verlassene Insel,
1893

Mein lieber Sohn Georg,

Ich bin ein alter Mann. Ich bin hier ganz allein, und mein Haus in der Nähe von Turmstadt steht leer. Ich habe ein Geheimnis. Ich bin sehr reich.
Du bekommst jetzt meinen ganzen Schatz. Du findest den ersten Hinweis im Blumenkohl-Haus. Du suchst die zwei Schiffe.

Leb wohl,
Tobias Blumenkohl

Whose is it?

In German, to say that something belongs to someone, you can either use the **genitive** case, or the preposition *von* (of, from) with the **dative** case. In the phrase "the young girl's boots", the owner is "the young girl", so the endings of these words in German change to show the appropriate case.

The genitive case

To say who something belongs to, you put the owner in the genitive case, e.g. *die Stiefel des Mädchens* (the girl's boots).

You can see the genitive forms of "the" and "a" in the grammar box on the right. Masculine and neuter nouns also add **s** or **es** on the end, e.g. *des Mädchens*. Adjectives usually add **en**. To put a name into the genitive case, you simply add an **s**, e.g. *Monikas Katze* (Monika's cat). If the name already ends in an **s** or a **z**, just add an apostrophe ('). In spoken German, you often avoid the genitive case and use *von* with the dative instead, e.g. *die Stiefel von dem Mädchen* (the girl's boots).

The dative case

This case is used after some prepositions (see page 40) and also whenever a noun is the indirect object, e.g. "cat" in "I'll give this milk to the cat". In the dative case, most plural nouns add **n** on the end, and adjectives add **en**. Here are the words for "the" and "a" in the dative.

"The" and "a" in the genitive and dative cases

	[m]	[f]	[n]	[pl]
genitive:	des	der	des	der
	eines	einer	eines	
dative:	dem	der	dem	den
	einem	einer	einem	

Gehören (to belong to)

This verb is another way to say whose something is. Like *von*, it is followed by the dative case. It is used far more than English uses "belong to", so when in German you say *Es gehört Tanja*, in English you would just say "It's Tanja's".

 Learning tip

Try learning the endings for the nominative, accusative, genitive and dative cases together as a chant. You'll find a complete list on page 96.

Fast Facts

In the singular, the German for my (*mein*), your (*dein*), his (*sein*), etc. have the same endings as *ein*. So you only have to learn the pattern once.

My, your, his, her...

The words for "my", "your", "his", etc., as in "my shirt", are a special kind of adjective, and in German they must agree with the noun they refer to. Here are the different forms in the nominative:

	[m] and [n]	[f] and [pl]
my	mein	meine
your	dein	deine
his/its	sein	seine
her/its	ihr	ihre
our	unser	unsere
your (plural)	euer	eure
their	ihr	ihre
your (polite)	Ihr	Ihre

e.g. *Deine Jacke ist rot.*
(Your jacket is red.)

Kleider

der Anzug(-¨e)	suit
der Gürtel(-)	belt
der Handschuh(-e)	glove
das Hemd(-en)	shirt
die Hose(-n)	trousers
der Hut(-¨e)	hat
die Jacke(-n)	jacket
die Jeans [pl]	jeans
das Kleid(-er)	dress
die Kleider [pl]	clothes
der Mantel(-¨)	coat
der Pulli(-s)	jumper
der Rock(-¨e)	skirt
die Sandale(-n)	sandal
der Schuh(-e)	shoe
die Shorts [pl]	shorts
die Socke(-n)	sock
der Stiefel(-)	boot
die Strumpfhose(-n)	tights
das Sweatshirt(-s)	sweatshirt
das T-Shirt(-s)	T-shirt
die Sportschuhe [pl]	trainers
tragen*	to wear

Wir tragen unsere neue Kleider.
We're wearing our new clothes.

mein T-Shirt

mein Pulli

mein Hemd

meine Jeans

meine Hose

meine Sportschuhe

meine Schuhe

The Blumenkohl treasure: chapter 4

Erich and Tanja arrive at the Blumenkohl house, where they are shown lots of interesting things and meet a very destructive goat in the garden. How silly of them to leave their bags on the steps outside...

New words

das Atelier(-s)	studio
das Bild(-er)	picture
die Brille(-n)	glasses
der Bruder(-̈)	brother
die Eltern [pl]	parents
das Fernglas(-̈er)	binoculars
der Freund(-e)	friend
der Großvater(-̈)	grandfather
der Hund(-e)	dog
die Katze(-n)	cat
die Mutter(-̈)	mother
der Nachbar(-n)	neighbour
das Porträt(-s)	portrait
der Untermieter(-)	lodger
die Ziege(-n)	goat
das Zimmer(-)	(bed)room
heißen*	to be called
dieser, diese, dieses	this, that
guten Tag	hello
Lieblings-	favourite
wem gehört/	whose
gehören?	is/are?

23

Telling people what to do

To tell someone what to do (for example, "Wait!") you use the imperative of the verb. In German, there are three main forms of the imperative: *du*, *ihr* and *Sie*. You can also use the verb *müssen* to tell someone that they "must" do something.

Making the imperative

To make the imperative in German, you start with the verb's present tense. For the *du* form, drop the *du* and the *-st* ending, so *du gehst* (you go) becomes *geh!* For the *ihr* form, drop the *ihr*, e.g. *geht!* For the *Sie* form, put the *Sie* after the verb, e.g. *gehen Sie!*

Du kommst becomes *Komm!* (Come!)

Useful imperatives

Here is a list of imperatives that are used very often. Most of them follow the normal pattern, but the imperative of the verb *sein* (to be) is completely irregular.

du form	ihr form	Sie form
pass auf!	passt auf!	passen Sie auf! (watch out)
bleib!	bleibt!	bleiben Sie! (stay, keep)
nimm!	nehmt!	nehmen Sie! (take)
gib!	gebt!	geben Sie! (give)
sei!	seid!	seien Sie! (be)

Saying "must"

Müssen is a useful irregular verb for saying what you must do. It is used with the infinitive of another verb, and this goes to the end of the sentence, e.g. *Ich muss brav sein.* (I must be good.)

Müssen (to have to, must)

ich muss	I must
du musst	you must
er/sie/es muss	he/she/it must
wir müssen	we must
ihr müsst	you must
sie müssen	they must
Sie müssen	you must

Sie müssen die Beschriftung lesen. You must read the label.

Fast facts

You can encourage your friends to do something with you by using the *wir* form of the imperative. Just put the *wir* after the verb, e.g. *Gehen wir ins Kino!* (**Let's go** to the cinema!)

Giving directions

The imperative is very useful for giving and understanding directions. Here is a list of direction words:

die Ampel(-n)	traffic lights
der Fußgänger-	pedestrian
überweg(-e)	crossing
die Kreuzung(-en)	crossroads
der Platz(-¨e)	square
die Straße(-n)	road, street
der Weg(-e)	path, lane, way
*fahren**	to go, to drive
*gehen**	to go, to walk
*nehmen**	to take
erst-[1]	first
zweit-[1]	second
dritt-[1]	third
viert-[1]	fourth
geradeaus	straight ahead
nach links	(to the) left
nach rechts	(to the) right
über	over
weiter	further

[1]You need to add endings to these adjectives, e.g. *die erste Straße links* (the first road on the left). See pages 12 and 96 for more about adjectives.

Using *man*

The German word *man* means "you" in the general sense of "people", "everyone" or "one". It is used a lot in German, and takes the same verb endings as *er/sie/es*:

e.g. *Man kann nie wissen.*
(You can never tell.)

Man muss im Voraus reservieren.
You must book in advance.

 Vorsicht!

• The German for "man" is *der Mann*. Try not to confuse it with *man* (you, people, one).

• When giving directions in German, you don't use the verb "carry on". Instead you say *Fahren/Gehen Sie immer geradeaus* which, word for word, means "Drive/Go always straight ahead".

Spielen wir Fußball!
Let's play football.

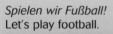

Spiel den Ball hierher!
Pass the ball here!

Renn!
Run!

Wir müssen gewinnen!
We must win!

The Blumenkohl treasure: chapter 5

The three friends are doing battle with Fresser, the neighbour's goat. They're having a tough time getting the animal back where it belongs.

That chore done, the three friends decide to visit an old church nearby. They go off on their bicycles, leaving the house unattended...

Geh nach links...

...und nimm den ersten Weg rechts.

Hüpfer, komm hierher!

Unknown to them, an unwelcome visitor arrives.

Das muss das Blumenkohl-Haus sein.

Ich muss diesen Hinweis schnell finden.

Zuerst muss ich meine Nagelfeile finden.

Sei ruhig!

Diese Schlösser müssen sehr alt sein.

New words

der Hinweis(-e)	clue, tip
die Höhle(-n)	cave
die Nagelfeile(-n)	nail file
das Schloss(-̈er)	lock
das Seil(-e)	rope
das Tor(-e)	gate
anschauen	to look at
aufpassen	to watch out, to be careful
sich beeilen	to hurry
bleiben*	to stay, to keep
einkaufen gehen*	to go shopping
kommen*	to come
müssen	to have to, must
schließen*	to close, to shut
warten	to wait
werfen*	to throw
ziehen*	to pull
alles	everything
bis später	see you later
brav	good, well behaved
fest	tight, hard
hierher	(to) here
immer	always
langsam	slow, slowly
richtig	right, correct
ruhig	quiet, calm
schnell	quickly, fast
sei!	be!
zuerst	first of all, at first

Asking questions

To ask a question in German, you simply change the order of the sentence by putting the subject after the verb. You can also use a question word at the beginning of the sentence.

Making questions

The German for "You have my jumper" is *Du hast meinen Pulli.* To make this sentence into a question, you simply turn the subject and verb around and say **Hast du** *meinen Pulli?* (Do you have my jumper?)

Haben Sie Roggenbrot?
Do you have any rye bread?

Question words

Question words, such as the ones listed below, go at the beginning of the sentence in German. They are followed by the verb and then the subject.

wie viel(e)?	how much/many?
wie?	how?
wo(hin)?	where (to)?
warum?	why?
wann?	when?
was?	what?
welcher?	which?/what?
wer?	who?

Welcher changes to match the noun that comes after it, and it follows the same pattern as *der/die/das/die* (see page 96):
e.g. W*elche Straße?* (Which road?)
Welches Sweatshirt willst du?
(Which sweatshirt do you want?)

Modal verbs

German has six irregular verbs known as modal verbs. These verbs indicate a mood, such as "wanting". The modal verbs are *wollen* (to want), *müssen* (must, to have to), *mögen* (to like), *können* (can, to be able to), *dürfen* (may, to be allowed to) and *sollen* (to be supposed to, to be meant to).

Modal verbs are very common in German. They are often used with another verb in the infinitive, which goes to the end of the sentence:

e.g. **Willst** *du Tennis* **spielen?**
(Do you want to play tennis?)
Ich **muss** *mein Zimmer* **aufräumen.**
(I have to tidy my room.)

Ich muss einen Fahrschein kaufen.
I have to buy a ticket.

Wann fährt der Zug?
When does the train leave?

The modal verb *sollen* is used for saying what you are "supposed" or "meant" to do:
e.g. *Ich soll um 9 Uhr ins Bett gehen.*
(I'm supposed to go to bed at 9 o'clock.)

You can also use *sollen* if you want to offer to do something:
e.g. *Soll ich mein Zimmer aufräumen?*
(Shall I tidy my room?)

Can I? May I?

To say "can" or "may" in German, you use the modal verbs *können* and *dürfen*. Both are used in questions to ask if you may do something, but *dürfen* is more polite:

e.g. **Kann** ich ins Kino gehen? (**Can** I go to the cinema?) **Darf** ich mal probieren? (**May** I have a taste?)

Fast facts

If you want to ask for something politely, use *ich möchte* (I would like), e.g. *Ich möchte ein Eis.* (I'd like an ice-cream.) *Ich möchte* is a special form of the modal verb *mögen* (to like).

Können (can)
Dürfen (may)

ich kann	I can
du kannst	you can
er/sie/es kann	he/she/it can
wir können	we can
ihr könnt	you can
sie können	they can
Sie können	you can
ich darf	I may
du darfst	you may
er/sie/es darf	he/she/it may
wir dürfen	we may
ihr dürft	you may
sie dürfen	they may
Sie dürfen	you may

Einkaufen gehen

der Apfel(-ˉ)	apple
die Apotheke(-n)	pharmacy
die Bäckerei(-en)	bakery
das Brot(-e)	bread
das Brötchen(-)	bread roll
das Eis	ice-cream
die Erdbeere(-n)	strawberry
das Geschäft(-e)	shop
das Kilo	kilo (of)
die Konditorei(-en)	cake shop
der Korb(-ˉe)	basket
der Kuchen(-)	cake
die Orange(-n)	orange
der Supermarkt(-ˉe)	supermarket
anprobieren	to try on
einkaufen gehen*	to go shopping
kosten	to cost
probieren	to try, to taste

Was kosten diese Schuhe?
What do these shoes cost?

Darf ich das T-Shirt da anprobieren?
May I try on that T-shirt?

The Blumenkohl treasure: chapter 6

Monika's mother, Heidrun, is doing her grocery shopping...

Meanwhile, Erich, Tanja and Monika have arrived at the church. While they're resting, Tanja remembers the letter that the man dropped at the café...

Monika knows that Tobias was her great-grandfather. After studying his letter to his son Georg, she realizes that it is the start of a trail of clues leading to hidden treasure.

First they will need to go back to the house to look at the two old pictures of ships...

New words

die Apotheke(-n)	pharmacy
der Brief(-e)	letter
der Krebs(-e)	crab
die Schatzsuche	treasure hunt
der Witz(-e)	joke
der Zauberer(-)	magician
erklären	to explain
echt	real, genuine
entschuldigen Sie	excuse me
geschlossen	closed
klasse!	great!
krank	ill

Negatives

In English, you make a sentence negative by using words such as "not", "don't" or "no". To make a German sentence negative, you use the words *nicht* (not) or *kein*, which means "not a", "not any" or "no". For example, *ich verstehe nicht* (I don't understand) and *ich habe keine Ahnung* (I have no idea).

Using *nicht*

Nicht usually comes at the end of a clause, e.g. *Ich mag Spinat nicht*. (I don't like spinach.)

Sometimes *nicht* comes **before** the end of the clause, for example:
• If there are two verbs in a sentence, *nicht* usually goes before the second one, e.g. *Ich will nicht tanzen*. (I don't want to dance.)
• If you use the verb *sein* (to be) plus an adjective or noun, *nicht* usually comes before that adjective or noun, e.g. *Es ist nicht kalt*. (It's not cold.)

Ich kann dieses Motorrad nicht reparieren.
I can't repair this motorbike.

Negative words

Here are some other negative words that can be used in German:
nie   never
niemand   nobody
nichts   nothing
Nie is used in the same way as *nicht*. *Niemand* and *nichts* can be either the subject or the object of a sentence.

You must not

To say that someone must not do something, in the sense that they are not allowed to, you use *dürfen*: e.g. *Du darfst nicht*. (You mustn't.) It is important not to use *müssen* (to have to, must) because *du musst nicht* means "you don't have to".

Niemand versteht mich!
Nobody understands me!

Using *kein*

In German, you don't usually say *nicht ein*. Instead, you use the word *kein* (not a, not any, no). *Kein* takes the same endings as *ein* and goes in the same place in the sentence:

e.g. *Das ist kein Hund*.
(That's not a dog.)
Ich habe keine Katze.
(I don't have a cat.)

Learning tip

If *nicht* comes before a particular word, then it usually makes just that word negative, rather than the whole sentence, e.g. *ich komme nicht heute* means "I'm not coming **today**". This suggests you might come on another day.

Saying that you know

German uses two different verbs to talk about "what" and "who" you know. To say that you know a fact (e.g. I know I have an exam tomorrow), you use the irregular verb *wissen*. To say that you know, or are acquainted with, a person or place, you use the verb *kennen*.

Wissen (to know)

ich weiß	I know
du weißt	you know
er/sie/es weiß	he/she/it knows
wir wissen	we know
ihr wisst	you know
sie wissen	they know
Sie wissen	you know

Fast facts

• In German, when a double "s" comes immediately after two vowels, it is always written "ß", as in *ich weiß*.

• The verb *kennen* uses the normal present tense verb endings, e.g. *ich kenne, du kennst, er kennt*, etc.

Mögen (to like)

ich mag	I like
du magst	you like
er/sie/es mag	he/she/it likes
wir mögen	we like
ihr mögt	you like
sie mögen	they like
Sie mögen	you like

Saying what you like

In German, there are many ways to say that you like something. The easiest is *ich mag*, from the modal verb *mögen* (to like):
e.g. *Ich mag Schokolade.*
(I like chocolate.)

Another way is to use *ich habe*, followed by the thing that you like, and then the word *gern*:
e.g. *Ich habe Hunde gern.*
(I like dogs.)

To say you like doing something, you also use *gern*. Just put *gern* after the verb:
e.g. *Ich spiele gern Fußball.*
(I like playing football.)

Wer gewinnt?
Who's winning?

Ich weiß es nicht.
I don't know.

Das ist nicht möglich!
That's not possible!

The Blumenkohl treasure: chapter 7

Heidrun arrives home with her groceries. She starts cooking without realizing there's someone in the house or, to be more precise, someone in her studio...

Die Tür ist nicht abgeschlossen.

Aber die Fahrräder sind nicht da.

Sei ruhig, Hüpfer! Du darfst nicht so laut bellen!

Was suchst du?

Es ist niemand da.

Da ist doch irgendwo ein Einbrecher!

Welche Schiffe? Es gibt hier keine Schiffe.

Guten Abend, Liebling. Guten Abend Uli.

Guten Abend, Schätzchen... Ach nein! Ich finde keine Kopfschmerztabletten.

Und weißt du warum? Die Apotheke ist geschlossen.

Ich habe nichts, keine Tabletten, keine Pflaster...

Monika, Erich and Tanja arrive home and head straight for the studio and the two paintings. The burglar makes a hasty retreat...

Hallo allerseits!

Ach! Schaut bloß nicht herüber.

Hier sind die zwei Schiffe.

Oh, da draußen ist ein Mann.

34

New words

der Einbrecher(-)	burglar
das Essen	food
die Kopfschmerz-tablette(-n)	headache tablet
das Pflaster(-)	sticking plaster
das Schiff(-e)	ship
die Tablette(-n)	pill, tablet
die Tür(-en)	door
bellen	to bark
finden*	to find
schauen	to look
abgeschlossen	locked
allerseits	everybody
bloß	merely, only, just
doch	yet, but
draußen	outside
es gibt	there is/are
fertig	ready
ganz	quite, exactly
gleich¹	(the) same
gleich²	immediately, right away
guten Abend	good evening
herüber	over here
irgendwo	somewhere
Liebling, Schätzchen	darling, dear
nichts	nothing
niemand	nobody
so laut	so loud(ly)

The first clue

Six missing items in the second picture are enough to tell the three friends where the next clue must be. They decide to go there the next day.

Picture one

Picture two

Can you spot which six items are missing in the second picture?
(The same items have already appeared in the story, on a sign over a door...)

Separable verbs

Some German verbs, known as separable verbs, are made up of a basic verb with an extra word joined on the front. The extra word is called a prefix. It often separates off from the verb and goes to the end of the sentence.

Using separable verbs

Zumachen (to close) is a separable verb made up of the basic verb *machen* and the prefix *zu*. When you conjugate the verb, *machen* and *zu* separate:
e.g. *Er **macht** die Tür **zu**.*
(He closes the door.)

Zumachen (to close)

ich mache zu	I close/am closing
du machst zu	you close
er/sie/es macht zu	he/she/it closes
wir machen zu	we close
ihr macht zu	you close
sie machen zu	they close
Sie machen zu	you close

If a separable verb comes at the end of a sentence, for example after a modal verb like *dürfen*, then the two parts join back together:
e.g. *Darf ich die Tür **zumachen**?*
(May I close the door?)

Ich habe meinen neuen Schmuck an.
I'm wearing my new jewellery.

Prefixes

To help you spot other separable verbs, here is a list of common prefixes:

Common prefixes

ab, an, auf, aus, ein, hinein, herein, her, hierher, hin, dahin, dorthin, los, mit, nach, weg, um, herum, zu

From now on, in the word lists, separable verbs are shown with an apostrophe (') between the prefix and the basic verb, e.g. *auf'passen*.

Pass auf! Du fährst hier falsch!
Watch out! You're going the wrong way!

Inseparable verbs

Some verbs may look separable, but not all prefixes separate from the verb they are with. Prefixes which stay with their basic verb include: *be-, emp-, ent-, er-, ge-, miss-, ver-,* and *zer-*:

e.g. *Ich empfehle dieses Restaurant.*
(I recommend this restaurant.)

Eating

To say what you're eating in German, you use the strong verb *essen*. In English, you sometimes use the verb "to have":
e.g. *Ich esse Pommes frites.*
(I'm having chips.)
You can also use *essen* with *gern* to say that you like a kind of food:
e.g. *Ich esse gern Käse.*
(I like cheese.)

Essen (to eat)

ich esse	I eat/am eating
du isst	you eat
er/sie/es isst	he/she/it eats
wir essen	we eat
ihr esst	you eat
sie essen	they eat
Sie essen	you eat

Fast facts

• To say you don't like something, you use *nicht gern*:
e.g. *Ich esse nicht gern Spinat.*
(I don't like spinach.)

• The *er* form of *essen* (*er isst*) sounds exactly the same as the *er* form of the verb *sein* (*er ist*).

Gehen or *fahren*?

The German verbs *gehen* and *fahren* both mean "to go", but *fahren* is used if you are taking transport, while *gehen* is used for going on foot.

e.g. *Franz fährt mit dem Bus.*
(Franz is going by bus.)
Claudia geht zu Fuß.
(Claudia is going on foot.)

Gehen and *fahren* are both strong verbs, but *fahren* adds an umlaut (¨) with *du* and *er/sie/es*.

Fahren (to go, to drive)

ich fahre	I go/am going
du fährst	you go
er/sie/es fährt	he/she/it goes
wir fahren	we go
ihr fahrt	you go
sie fahren	they go
Sie fahren	you go

Der Kellner trägt zwei Eis herein!
The waiter's bringing in two ice-creams!

Er kommt vielleicht mit unserem Nachtisch an!
Maybe he's arriving with our dessert!

The next day, Erich, Tanja and Monika have arrived at the *Magician's Inn*, in search of the next clue. Monika has her camera with her. But finding what they're looking for isn't easy with all those people around, and unknown to the three friends they are being watched...

Gehen wir einkaufen, Liebling.

Warte! Ich lese meine Zeitung.

Helgas Zug kommt bald an.

Wann fangen die Prüfungen an?

Fang schon an!

New words

das Foto(-s)	photo
das Gemüse	vegetables
der Käse(-)	cheese
das Kind(-er)	kid, child
Pommes frites [pl]	chips
die Prüfung(-en)	exam
die Schüssel(-n)	bowl
die Suppe(-n)	soup
die Zeitung(-en)	newspaper
der Zug(-̈e)	train
ab'hauen	to clear off
an'fangen*	to start, to begin
an'kommen*	to arrive
Fotos machen	to take photos
herein'tragen*	to carry in
lesen*	to read
reichen	to be enough
stören	to annoy, to bother
also	well then
bald	soon
der/die/das nächste	the next
doof	stupid
jetzt	now
nie	never
schon	already
überhaupt	anyhow, at all

39

Prepositions

Prepositions are words like "in", "on", "to" or "from". In German, the noun or pronoun that follows a preposition usually goes into the accusative or dative case.

With the accusative

bis	until, as far as
durch	through
entlang	along(side)
für	for
gegen	against, towards
ohne	without
um	around, at

With the dative

aus	out of, from
bei	at X's (house)
gegenüber	opposite
mit	with
nach	after, to
seit	since
von	from, of, by
zu	to, to X's (house)

Accusative or dative

an	at, on
auf	on, onto, on top of
hinter	behind
in	in, into
neben	next to, beside
über	over, across
unter	under, among
vor	in front of, before
zwischen	between

Which case?

The pink box lists prepositions which are followed by the accusative case and those followed by the dative case. For instance, you would say *durch den Wald* (through the forest) but *aus dem Wald* (out of the forest).

The nine prepositions listed at the bottom of the box are sometimes followed by the accusative and sometimes by the dative. If the sentence involves movement, use the accusative; if there is no movement, use the dative.
e.g. *Er geht hinter **das** Haus.*
(He's going behind the house.)
*Er ist hinter **dem** Haus.*
(He is behind the house.)

Ich fahre in die Stadtmitte.
I'm going into the town centre.

Vorsicht!

- In German you don't always use the same preposition as in English. For instance, "**by** train" is *mit dem Zug.*

- The preposition *entlang* goes after the noun, e.g. *den Fluss entlang* (along the river).

Learning tip

Try learning the three lists of prepositions in this order, as a chant: *durch, für, gegen, ohne, um, entlang;* then *mit, nach, von, zu, aus, bei, seit, gegenüber;* and *in, an, auf, über, unter, hinter, neben, zwischen, vor.*

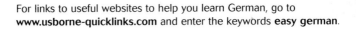
Making contractions

A contraction is when two words are shortened, such as "don't" instead of "do not". In German, you can make contractions from some prepositions and the word for "the". Here are the most common ones:

an das	-	ans
an dem	-	am
auf das	-	aufs
bei dem	-	beim
in das	-	ins
in dem	-	im
von dem	-	vom
zu dem	-	zum
zu der	-	zur

Using *bei* and *zu*

The German for "at home" is *zu Hause*". If you want to say "at my house" or "at mine" you use *bei* with the dative pronoun *mir* (me): *bei mir*. You can also use *bei* with someone's name and say *bei Ralf* (at Ralf's). To say that you are going to someone's house, you use *zu* followed by the name: e.g. *Wir gehen zu Ralf.* (We're going to Ralf's.)

Some country names

Australien	Australia
Deutschland	Germany
England	England
Frankreich	France
Irland	Ireland
Italien	Italy
Österreich	Austria
Schottland	Scotland
die Schweiz	Switzerland
Spanien	Spain
die Vereinigten Staaten	United States
Wales	Wales

The continents

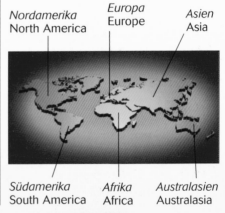

Nordamerika
North America

Europa
Europe

Asien
Asia

Südamerika
South America

Afrika
Africa

Australasien
Australasia

Zwei Mädchen sitzen auf dem Sand am Meer.
Two girls are sitting on the sand at the seaside.

Silke ist unter dem Sonnenschirm.
Silke is under the parasol.

Sie sitzt neben ihrer Freundin.
She's sitting beside her friend.

41

The Blumenkohl treasure: chapter 9

Outside the inn, Tanja spots the man who has been following them. He is on his way out. Erich, Tanja and Monika realize they have seen him before. He too must be after the treasure.

They have to lose him quickly, so they head for the harbour.

New words

die Antwort(-en)	answer
der Ausgang(-˙e)	exit
die Bank(-˙e)	bench
der Baum(-˙e)	tree
der Brunnen(-)	fountain
die Frage(-n)	question
der Garten(-˙)	garden
das Gebäude(-)	building
die Glatze(-n)	bald head/patch
der Hügel(-)	hill
der Kai(-e or -s)	quay
die Kuh(-˙e)	cow
der Kumpel(-)	mate, good friend
die Lupe(-n)	magnifying glass
das Netz(-e)	net
die Schule(-n)	school
der Speicher(-)	attic
der Zettel(-)	note
legen	to put (lay down)
stehen*	to stand
wohnen	to live
der-/die-/dasselbe	the (very) same
oje!	oh dear! oh no!
schon gut	all right, OK
zu Hause	at home

Using the magnifying glass, Erich, Tanja and Monika look at the note that Erich found at the inn. At first it is very puzzling, but with the help of Monika's photograph of the painted seat at the inn, they work out where to go next.

Can you figure out where the three friends must go next? (Try and find a building on this page which matches the answers to Tobias Blumenkohl's questions. The first answer is *unter dem Baum*.)

Reflexive verbs

Reflexive verbs are verbs which include a pronoun, such as *mich* (myself) or *dich* (yourself). The pronoun "reflects back" the subject of the verb, which means that the subject and the object are the same, for example "I wash myself".

Forming reflexive verbs

German reflexive verbs follow the same pattern as ordinary verbs, except that there is a special reflexive pronoun after the verb. The pronouns are:

mich	myself
dich	yourself
sich	himself, herself, itself
uns	ourselves
euch	yourselves
sich	themselves
sich	yourself, yourselves

Note that German reflexive verbs are always accompanied by a pronoun, while in English the reflexive pronoun is optional.

Sich waschen (to wash oneself, to have a wash)

ich wasche mich	I wash (myself)
du wäschst dich	you wash (yourself)
er/sie/es wäscht sich	he/she/it washes (him-/her-/itself)
wir waschen uns	we wash (ourselves)
ihr wascht euch	you wash (yourselves)
sie waschen sich	they wash (themselves)
Sie waschen sich	you wash (yourself/-selves)

Useful reflexive verbs

sich amüsieren	to enjoy oneself
sich an'ziehen	to get dressed
sich ärgern	to get annoyed
sich aus'ruhen	to have a rest, to relax
sich aus'ziehen	to get undressed
sich beeilen	to hurry up
sich befinden	to be, to be found, to be situated
sich beruhigen	to calm down
sich duschen	to have a shower
sich fühlen	to feel
sich rasieren	to shave
sich setzen	to sit down
sich um'ziehen	to get changed
sich verstecken	to hide (oneself)
sich waschen	to wash (oneself)

Some reflexive verbs are also separable verbs, e.g. *sich anziehen* (to get dressed). As with ordinary separable verbs, the two parts of the verb split up. So, "I get dressed" is *ich ziehe mich an*.

Giving orders

Reflexive verbs make their imperatives in the same way as ordinary verbs, but you keep *dich*, *euch* and *sich*. The imperatives of the verb *sich beeilen* are:

Beeil dich!	Hurry up!
Beeilt euch!	Hurry up!
Beeilen Sie sich!	Hurry up!

Fast facts

• German has lots more reflexive verbs than English. Verbs such as *sich ausruhen* (to rest) don't seem reflexive at all in English.

• The word *sich* can mean "himself", "herself", "itself", "oneself", "themselves", "yourself" or "yourselves"!

Saying you're interested

To say that you're interested in something, you use the reflexive verb *sich interessieren für*:
e.g. *Ich interessiere mich für Tennis.*
(I'm interested in tennis.)

Ich interessiere mich sehr für Katzen.
I'm really interested in cats.

Spot the difference

With reflexive verbs, the subject and object are the same:
e.g. *Er wäscht sich.*
(He washes himself.)

With ordinary verbs, the subject and object are different:
e.g. *Er wäscht das Auto.*
(He washes the car.)

Who and which

In German, to say "the man **who**..." or "the cat **which**...", you use *der, die* or *das*, depending on the gender of whatever you're referring to. You put a comma in front, and the verb goes to the end of the clause:
e.g. *Der Mann, **der** da drüben sitzt,...*
(The man **who** is sitting over there...)
*Die Katze, **die** auf dem Bett liegt,...*
(The cat **which** is lying on the bed...)

If the word for "who(m)" or "which" is the direct object, rather than the subject, it goes into the accusative:
e.g. *Der Mann, **den** ich gut kenne,...*
(The man **who(m)** I know well...)

Unlike in English, you cannot omit the word for "who" or "which" in German.

Telling the time

To answer *Wie viel Uhr ist es?* (What time is it?) you say *Es ist...* (It is...):

...Mittag/Mitternacht

...Viertel vor eins

...zehn vor acht

...halb elf (half way to eleven)

...zwanzig nach elf

...drei Uhr

The Blumenkohl treasure: chapter 10

Erich, Tanja and Monika are at the school, looking for the next clue. They creep past the classrooms where different lessons are going on. Unknown to the three friends, they are still being followed...

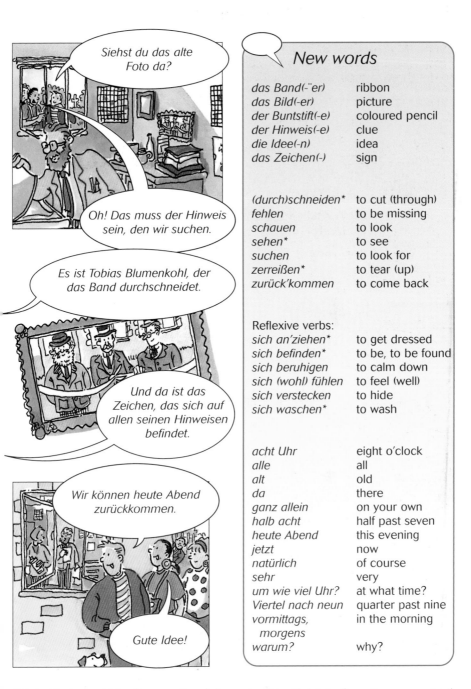

New words

das Band(-¨er)	ribbon
das Bild(-er)	picture
der Buntstift(-e)	coloured pencil
der Hinweis(-e)	clue
die Idee(-n)	idea
das Zeichen(-)	sign

(durch)schneiden*	to cut (through)
fehlen	to be missing
schauen	to look
sehen*	to see
suchen	to look for
zerreißen*	to tear (up)
zurück'kommen	to come back

Reflexive verbs:

sich an'ziehen*	to get dressed
sich befinden*	to be, to be found
sich beruhigen	to calm down
sich (wohl) fühlen	to feel (well)
sich verstecken	to hide
sich waschen*	to wash

acht Uhr	eight o'clock
alle	all
alt	old
da	there
ganz allein	on your own
halb acht	half past seven
heute Abend	this evening
jetzt	now
natürlich	of course
sehr	very
um wie viel Uhr?	at what time?
Viertel nach neun	quarter past nine
vormittags, morgens	in the morning
warum?	why?

Erich, Tanja and Monika must wait for school to finish before they can sneak back to look at the old photograph.

47

Saying what you're doing

There are two verbs for "to do" in German: the weak verb *machen* and the irregular verb *tun*. *Machen* is more common and can also mean "to make". *Tun* has other meanings too, such as "to put".

Tun (to do)

ich tu(e)	I do/am doing
du tust	you do
er/sie/es tut	he/she/it does
wir tun	we do
ihr tut	you do
sie tun	they do
Sie tun	you do

Was tust du hier?
What are you doing here?

Tun and machen phrases

es tut mir Leid - I'm sorry
was tun? - what can be done?
was tuts? - what does it matter?

ein Foto machen - to take a photo
Pause machen - to have a break
eine Party machen - to have a party
eine Prüfung machen - to do an exam
es macht nichts - it doesn't matter
machs gut! - all the best!
machs kurz! - make it short!

More about tun

Another meaning of *tun* is "to put":
e.g. *Ich tu(e) das in meine Tasche.*
(I'll put that in my bag.)
The *-e* ending on the *ich* form of *tun* is often omitted.

German word order

In a simple German sentence, the verb must be the second element. This means you often have to turn the subject and verb around:
e.g. *Im Sommer **spiele ich** Tennis.*
(In the summer I play tennis.)
Here are some examples:

Es ist sonnig heute.
It's sunny today.

Heute ist es heiß.
It's hot today.

In Kanada ist es kalt.
It's cold in Canada.

Hier ist es windig.
It's windy here.

Word order in clauses

A clause is a section of a sentence that has a subject and a verb (see page 7). If a German clause begins with a word such as *weil* (because) or *dass* (that), then the verb goes to the end of the clause:
e.g. *...weil ich heute Tennis **spiele**.*
(...because I'm playing tennis today.)
See page 115 for a list of other words that send the verb to the end of the clause.

More about clauses

In German, you put a comma on either side of each clause:
e.g. *Ich gähne, weil ich müde bin, aber ich kann nicht schlafen.*
(I'm yawning because I'm tired, but I can't sleep.)
If there is a modal verb plus an infinitive, the modal verb goes last:
e.g. *...weil er nicht fahren **kann**.*
(...because he can't drive.)

> *Ich kann nicht schlafen, weil es so viel Lärm gibt!*
> I can't sleep because there's so much noise!

Using *um...zu*

The German for "to/in order to" is *um...zu*. It is always used with an infinitive. You start the phrase with *um*, and put *zu* just before the infinitive at the end:

e.g. *Sie gehen zum Strand, **um** in der Sonne **zu** liegen.* (They go to the beach in order to sunbathe.)

When the infinitive is a separable verb, you put *zu* between the prefix and the main part of the verb:
e.g. *Wir fahren nach Frankfurt, um Erich am Bahnhof ab**zu**holen.*
(We're going to Frankfurt to pick Erich up at the station.)

> *Und es ist toll, dass die Sonne scheint.*
> And it's great that the sun is shining.

> *Wir haben Glück, dass es so viel Schnee gibt.*
> We're lucky that there's so much snow.

49

Before Erich, Tanja and Monika return to the school, the bald man pulls off a neat bit of impersonation and gets away with the photo...

Weil das da seine Aktentasche ist.

New words

das Fotokopier-gerät(-e)	photocopier
der Kommissar(-e)	police inspector
der Mechaniker(-)	mechanic
die Polizei-wache(-n)	police station
das Teil(-e)	part
ab'geben*	to hand in
hinein'kommen*	to get in
verpacken	to wrap (up)
zu'machen	to close, to shut
dumm	stupid
gerade, eben	just
kaputt	broken
morgen früh	tomorrow morning
na (gut/schön)	well, OK
woher?	where from?, how?
ziemlich	fairly, quite

Na schön, wir gehen zur Polizeiwache, um die Tasche abzugeben.

Outside the police station...

Sie ist zu.

Na gut, dann müssen wir morgen früh zurückkommen.

Kennst du den Kommissar?

Ja... Er ist ziemlich nett.

51

Pronouns

A pronoun is a word that replaces a noun, such as "he" instead of "John" and "it" instead of "the car". *Ich, du, er, sie, es, wir, ihr, sie* and *Sie* are all nominative pronouns because they replace the subject of the sentence. Pronouns can also be in the accusative or dative case. For example, in the sentence *Er gibt es mir* (He gives it to me), *Er* is nominative, *es* is accusative and *mir* is dative.

Accusative pronouns

Here's a list of German pronouns in the accusative case:

mich	me
dich	you
ihn	him/it
sie	her/it
es	it
uns	us
euch	you
sie	them
Sie	you

e.g. *Jens isst es.* (Jens is eating it.)

You use these pronouns for the **direct object** of a sentence. For instance, in the sentence *Jens isst ein Eis* (Jens is eating an ice-cream), the direct object is *ein Eis* and it can be replaced by *es*. You also use these pronouns after prepositions which take the accusative case, e.g. *ein Eis für mich* (an ice-cream for me).

The accusative pronouns *mich, dich, uns* and *euch* are exactly the same as the pronouns used with reflexive verbs (see page 44), e.g. *ich wasche mich* (I wash myself).

Dative pronouns

You use a dative pronoun for the **indirect object** of a sentence. Here are the dative pronouns in German:

mir	(to) me
dir	(to) you
ihm	(to) him/it
ihr	(to) her/it
ihm	(to) it
uns	(to) us
euch	(to) you
ihnen	(to) them
Ihnen	(to) you

So the sentence *Ich gebe Jens ein Eis* (I give Jens an ice-cream) can be shortened to *Ich gebe **ihm** ein Eis* (I give **him** an ice-cream). You also use these pronouns after prepositions that take the dative.

Dative reflexive pronouns

In German, to say "I wash (myself)", you use the reflexive verb *sich waschen* and say *ich wasche mich*. *Mich* is known as a reflexive pronoun and it is in the accusative case, because "myself" is the direct object of the sentence.

But if you say "I wash my hands", it is your hands which are the direct object. The reflexive pronoun becomes dative and you say *Ich wasche **mir** die Hände*. The dative reflexive pronouns are: *mir, dir, sich, uns, euch, sich* and *sich*.

Word order with pronouns

If you use an accusative pronoun (the direct object) and a dative pronoun (the indirect object) together, you put the accusative pronoun first:

e.g. *Reich es mir!*
(Pass it to me!)
Ich zeige es ihnen.
(I'll show it to them.)

Die Stewardess gibt Ralf die Bonbons.
(The stewardess gives Ralf the sweets.)
OR
Sie gibt sie ihm. (She gives them to him.)

If you have a mix of nouns and pronouns, then the pronoun usually comes first:

e.g. *Ich gebe meiner Schwester ein Geschenk.*
(I give my sister a present.)

*Ich gebe **ihr** ein Geschenk.*
(I give **her** a present.)

*Ich gebe **es** meiner Schwester.*
(I give **it** to my sister.)

With it, under it, on it...

If a preposition is followed by the words "it" or "them", in German you can just put *da-* (or *dar-* before a vowel) in front of the preposition:

e.g. *Ich sitze auf dem Tisch.*
(I'm sitting on the table.)
*Ich sitze **darauf**.* (I'm sitting **on it**.)

You can only do this when you are referring to things, and not people or animals.

Willst du diesen Brief noch?
Do you still want this letter?

Nein, ich bin damit fertig.
No, I'm finished with it.

 Vorsicht!

To use the correct German pronoun, you need to understand the cases. If a pronoun is the subject of the sentence, use the nominative case (*ich, du, er* etc.). If it is the direct object, use the accusative case (*mich, dich, ihn* etc.). If it is the indirect object, use the dative case (*mir, dir, ihm* etc.).

Magst du diese Musik?
Do you like this music?

Willst du mit mir tanzen?
Do you want to dance with me?

Ich finde sie echt cool!
I think it's really cool!

Nein, danke! Lass mich in Ruhe!
No, thanks! Leave me alone!

Erich, Tanja and Monika realize that in order to continue the hunt, they must first find the bald man. Perhaps his briefcase might be of some help...

After dinner...

Ein Tagebuch, eine Zeitung...

Aber schaut darunter... Da sind Papierschnitzel.

Es ist eine zerrissene Postkarte.

Aber können wir sie noch lesen?

New words

die Adresse(-n)	address
die Eltern [pl]	parents
das Papier(-e)	paper
die Polizei	police
der Schnitzel(-)	bit, scrap
das Tagebuch(-¨er)	diary
die Taschenlampe(-n)	torch, flashlight
die Zeitung(-en)	newspaper
bitten* um	to ask for
empfehlen*	to recommend
erzählen	to tell, to talk
lesen*	to read
verstecken	to hide
zeigen	to show
alles	everything
fertig	ready
frei	free
jedenfalls	anyhow
ruhig	quiet
schöne Ferien!	(have a) nice holiday!
vielen Dank	many thanks
vielleicht	maybe
wahrscheinlich	probably
zerrissen	torn up
zuerst	first, firstly

The torn postcard provides vital information for Erich, Tanja and Monika, once they have worked out how the pieces join together.

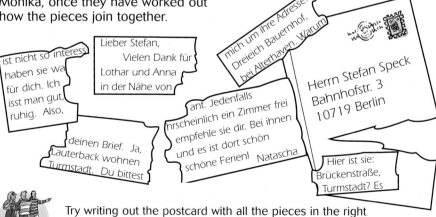

ist nicht so interess haben sie wa für dich. Ich isst man gut, ruhig. Also,

Lieber Stefan, Vielen Dank für Lothar und Anna in der Nähe von

mich um Ihre Adresse. Dreieich Bauernhof, bei Alterhaven. Warum

deinen Brief. Ja, Lauterback wohnen Turmstadt. Du bittest

ant. Jedenfalls hrscheinlich ein Zimmer frei empfehle sie dir. Bei ihnen und es ist dort schön schöne Ferien! Natascha

Herrn Stefan Speck Bahnhofstr. 3 10719 Berlin

Hier ist sie: Brückenstraße, Turmstadt? Es

Try writing out the postcard with all the pieces in the right order. Can you figure out what it says?

The imperfect tense

In German, there are two different tenses you can use to describe what you did in the past: the imperfect tense and the perfect tense (see pages 64-72). The imperfect tense is mainly used in formal writing, for example in books and newspapers. However, with some very common verbs you use the imperfect even in everyday speech.

Making the imperfect

Weak verbs, such as *spielen* (to play) and *machen* (to do), follow a regular pattern in the imperfect tense. To form the imperfect of a weak verb, you take the infinitive (e.g. *spielen*) and remove the *-en*, leaving the stem *spiel-*. Then, you add the imperfect tense endings:

Spielen (imperfect tense)

ich spiel**te**	I played/was playing
du spiel**test**	you played/were playing
er/sie/es spiel**te**	he/she/it played/was playing
wir spiel**ten**	we played/were playing
ihr spiel**tet**	you played/were playing
sie spiel**ten**	they played/were playing
Sie spiel**ten**	you played/were playing

Wo warst du gestern Abend um neun Uhr?
Where were you last night at nine o'clock?

Äh...ich war im Kino. Er...I was at the cinema.

Two useful imperfects

The two verbs that are used most frequently in the imperfect tense are the irregular verbs *haben* (to have) and *sein* (to be). It is normal to use the imperfect for these, even in everyday speech.

Haben (imperfect tense)

ich hatte	I had
du hattest	you had
er/sie/es hatte	he/she/it had
wir hatten	we had
ihr hattet	you had
sie hatten	they had
Sie hatten	you had

Sein (imperfect tense)

ich war	I was
du warst	you were
er/sie/es war	he/she/it was
wir waren	we were
ihr wart	you were
sie waren	they were
Sie waren	you were

Fast facts

If the stem of a weak verb ends in *-t*, you add an extra **e** before the imperfect endings, e.g. *du arbeit**e**test* (you worked).

Strong verbs

Strong verbs have an irregular stem in the imperfect tense. For example, the imperfect stem of *singen* (to sing) is *sang-*. These stems need to be learned, and you'll find a list on pages 114-115. In the imperfect, you add no endings to the stem of the *ich* and the *er* forms. For the rest, you add the endings shown here:

ich sang	I sang
du sangst	you sang
er/sie/es sang	he/she/it sang
wir sangen	we sang
ihr sangt	you sang
sie sangen	they sang
Sie sangen	you sang

There was...

To say, "there was" or "there were" in German, you use the imperfect tense of the strong verb *geben*. The phrase *es gibt* (there is/are) becomes *es gab* (there was/were).

Mixed verbs

German has a few verbs that are a mixture between strong and weak verbs. They are known as mixed verbs. In the imperfect tense, mixed verbs have an irregular stem, like strong verbs, but they add the same endings as weak verbs. There's a list of mixed verbs on page 115. Here's a useful one - *bringen* (to bring):

ich brachte	I brought
du brachtest	you brought
er/sie/es brachte	he/she/it brought
wir brachten	we brought
ihr brachtet	you brought
sie brachten	they brought
Sie brachten	you brought

Modal verbs

One group of verbs commonly used in the imperfect tense are the modal verbs, such as *müssen* (to have to) and *können* (to be able to). Most modal verbs have irregular stems in the imperfect, but they add weak endings (see page 113).

Heinrich sieht sich einige alte Fotos an.
Heinrich is looking at some old photos.

Hier war ich mit meinen Freunden am Meer.
Here, I was at the seaside with my friends.

Wir hatten viel Spaß auf dem Campingplatz.
We had lots of fun at the campsite.

The Blumenkohl treasure: chapter 13

The next morning, they take the briefcase to the police, along with the photo of the bald man which Monika took at the harbour. But they don't get the response they were expecting...

Also, wo war diese Aktentasche?

Und warum wart ihr dort?

Sie war auf dem Kopiergerät in der Schule.

Weil wir einen Schatz suchen.

Ja, und in der Schule war ein Hinweis.

Welcher Schatz?

Er gehört meiner Familie.

Ach so, ich verstehe. Und dieser Gauner will ihn stehlen.

Genau! Der Hinweis ist ein altes Foto.

Gestern Abend war das Foto nicht mehr da...

...aber die Aktentasche vom Gauner war da.

Sie gehört höchstwahrscheinlich dem Lehrer.

Aber nein, der Gauner hatte sie vorher.

Das reicht! Geht jetzt nach Hause.

After the trio have left the office...

Bringen Sie diese Aktentasche schnell zur Schule zurück.

New words

die Aktentasche(-n)	briefcase
die Familie(-n)	family
der Gauner(-)	crook, swindler
der Lehrer(-)	teacher
der Schatz(-¨e)	treasure
die Tasche(-)	bag, pocket
gehören [+ dat]	to belong to
stehlen*	to steal, to rob
verstehen*	to understand
weiter'machen	to continue
zurück'bringen	to bring, to take back
dort	there
genau	exactly
gestern Abend	yesterday evening
glücklicherweise	luckily
(höchst-) wahrscheinlich	(most) probably
jetzt	now
nach Hause	home
nicht mehr	no longer
noch	still
ohne	without
schnell	quick, quickly
(so ein) Pech!	(what) bad luck!
vorher	before(hand)

Pech! Aber wir können ohne die Polizei weitermachen.

Glücklicherweise kennen wir die Adresse von dem Mann mit der Glatze.

Oh, schaut mal! Ich habe noch das Tagebuch, das in der Aktentasche war.

Es war in meiner Tasche.

Using adverbs

Adverbs are words like "slowly" or "badly" that give extra meaning to a verb. There are three main types:
- adverbs of **time** tell you **when** the action happens;
- adverbs of **manner** describe **how** the action happens;
- adverbs of **place** indicate **where** the action happens.

Adjective or adverb?

In English, you can turn many adjectives into adverbs by adding "-ly" on the end, e.g. "slow" and "slowly". But German adjectives can be used as adverbs exactly as they are, without making any changes at all. So *langsam* can mean "slow" or "slowly", and *schnell* can mean "quick" or "quickly":
e.g. *Das Auto fährt langsam.*
(The car goes slowly.)
Unlike adjectives, you don't add any endings to German adverbs.

Ich fahre schnell!
I'm going quickly!

Spotting adverbs

Although German adjectives can also be used as adverbs, there are lots of German adverbs that can't be used as adjectives. Quite a few of these end in *-weise*, such as *normalerweise* (normally) or *glücklicherweise* (luckily). You can see a list of common adverbs in the box on the right.

Useful adverbs

Time
heute	today
gestern	yesterday
gestern Abend	yesterday evening
heute Abend	this evening
morgen	tomorrow
vormittags	in the morning(s)
nachmittags	in the afternoon(s)
abends	in the evening(s)
jetzt	now
später	later
vorher	before(hand)
schon	already
manchmal	sometimes
oft	often
immer	always, still

Manner
viel	a lot
selten	seldom, rarely
genau	exactly
glücklicherweise	luckily, fortunately
normalerweise	usually, normally
vielleicht	maybe, perhaps
fast	almost, nearly
wahrscheinlich	probably
wirklich	really

Place
hier	here
dort (drüben)	(over) there
dahin	(to) there
weit	far
überall	everywhere
nach Hause	(to) home
zu Hause	at home
irgendwo	somewhere
nirgendwo	nowhere

Phrases using adverbs

Below is a list of useful phrases that contain adverbs:

bis jetzt	so far
jetzt oder nie!	(it's) now or never!
bis morgen	see you tomorrow
bis später	see you later
ich bin nicht von gestern	I wasn't born yesterday
immer wieder	again and again
nur immer zu!	keep it up!
wie immer	as usual
wirklich und wahrhaftig	really and truly
hoffentlich nicht	I hope not
nicht unbedingt	not necessarily
hier und da	here and there
das Haus hier	this house
überall in der Welt	all over the world
weit und breit	for miles around

Adverbs and word order

If you use more than one adverb in a sentence, then the adverbs have to go in a particular order:

   1   2   3
Time - Manner - Place

So if you want to say that you are going "there" "quickly" "tomorrow", you would say: *Ich fahre morgen* (**time**) *schnell* (**manner**) *dahin* (**place**). If you only use two of the three types of adverb, you still have to put them in the right order.

If you start a sentence with an adverb, such as "today" or "sometimes", remember that the verb has to come next, before the subject:

e.g. *Heute **fahre ich** ans Meer.*
(I'm going to the seaside today.)

Er spielt hervorragend Saxofon.
He plays the saxophone brilliantly.

Seine Finger bewegen sich schnell.
His fingers move quickly.

Er schlägt kräftig.
He hits hard.

Manchmal spielt er zu leise.
Sometimes he plays too softly.

The Blumenkohl treasure: chapter 14

After leaving the police station, Erich finds a note and an interesting magazine cutting in the bald man's diary. It seems that he has recently been involved in illegal activities...

Seltene Vögel der Seltnafugal-Inseln

Vor hundert Jahren gab es viele blaue Papageien auf den Seltnafugal-Inseln. Die Einwohner beteten sie an und bauten Tempel zu ihren Ehren.

Diese Vögel findet man nun sehr selten, und man darf sie nicht fangen. Letztes Jahr konnte man hin und wieder einige auf einer entlegenen, verlassenen Insel namens Kuckuck sehen.

Herr Speck,

Besorgen Sie mir ein Paar blaue Papageien für meine Sammlung. Ihr Lohn: 15.000 Euro.

Frau Eule

Mensch!
Die Seltnafugal-Inseln...
Mein Urgroßvater ging
oft dahin, um die
Pflanzen anzusehen.

Er war Botaniker.

Und der
Mann mit der
Glatze war auf dieser
Inselgruppe, um
Papageien zu
stehlen.

Kommt schon.
Ich will euch etwas zu
Hause zeigen.

Back at home, Monika shows Erich and Tanja a very old letter written to her grandfather, Georg. It's from the governor of the Seltnafugal islands. It tells how her great-grandfather, Tobias, disappeared on one of the islands.

Seltnafugalstadt

Sehr geehrter Herr,
Leider ist Ihr Vater wahrscheinlich tot.
Er kannte unsere Inseln gut, aber zur Zeit
seines Verschwindens suchte er Pflanzen
auf gefährlichen, entlegenen Inseln. Er
arbeitete mit zwei Kollegen zusammen. Sie
hatten ein gutes Boot, aber es herrschte
die Sturmzeit.
Pedro Peperoni
Gouverneur der Seltnafugal-Inseln

New words

der Botaniker(-)	botanist
der Einwohner(-)	inhabitant
der Euro(-)	euro (currency)
die Inselgruppe(-n)	(group of) islands
das Jahr(-e)	year
der Kollege(-n)	colleague
der Lohn(-"e)	wage, fee
das Paar(-e)	pair
der Papagei(-en)	parrot
die Pflanze(-n)	plant
die Sammlung(-en)	collection
die Sturmzeit(-en)	stormy season
der Tempel(-)	temple
der Urgroßvater(-")	disappearance
das Verschwinden	great-grandfather
an'beten	to worship
arbeiten	to work
aus'sehen*	to seem, to look
bauen	to build
besorgen	to get, to acquire
fangen*	to catch
herrschen	to be (weather)
entlegen	remote, isolated
gefährlich	dangerous
hin und wieder	now and again
leider	unfortunately
letzt- [+ ending]	last
Mensch!	Hey! Wow! Man!
namens	named
nun	now
sehr geehrter	dear (formal)
selten	rare, scarce
tot	dead
zu ihren Ehren	in their honour
vor	ago
zur Zeit	at the time

The perfect tense

The perfect tense is the tense that is most often used in everyday German to describe what you did, or "have done", in the past. For example, to say "I played tennis yesterday" or "I've finished my homework" in German, you normally use the perfect tense. The other past tense - the imperfect - is mainly used in formal, written German.

How to form the perfect

The perfect tense is made up of two parts: the present tense of *haben* (or sometimes *sein*) and a special form of the verb you are using, called the past participle:

e.g. *Ich **habe** Tennis **gespielt**.*
(I played tennis.)
*Ralf **hat** ein neues T-Shirt **gekauft**.*
(Ralf bought a new T-shirt.)

The past participle (e.g. *gespielt* or *gekauft*) goes at the end of the clause. Most verbs form the perfect tense with *haben* (see page 68 to find out about verbs that use *sein*).

Weak verbs

It's easy to form the past participle of a weak verb. You simply take the infinitive (e.g. *machen*), add *ge-* in front, and replace the *-en* at the end with a *-t*. For example:

machen (to make)	-	***gemacht***
wohnen (to live)	-	***gewohnt***
kaufen (to buy)	-	***gekauft***

Wohin habe ich meine Schlüssel gesteckt? (Where have I put my keys?)

Was hast du gestern Abend gemacht?
What did you do yesterday evening?

Ich habe Musik gehört.
I listened to music.

Strong verbs

Strong verbs have an irregular past participle (see pages 114-115 for a list of these verbs). Strong past participles end in *-en*, and most of them begin with *ge-*. Here are some of the most useful ones:

beginnen (to begin)	*begonnen*
essen (to eat)	*gegessen*
finden (to find)	*gefunden*
geben (to give)	*gegeben*
helfen (to help)	*geholfen*
lesen (to read)	*gelesen*
nehmen (to take)	*genommen*
schlafen (to sleep)	*geschlafen*
schreiben (to write)	*geschrieben*
sehen (to see)	*gesehen*
sprechen (to speak)	*gesprochen*
stehlen (to steal)	*gestohlen*
treffen (to meet)	*getroffen*
trinken (to drink)	*getrunken*
vergessen (to forget)	*vergessen*
verlieren (to lose)	*verloren*
waschen (to wash)	*gewaschen*

Mixed verbs

German has a small number of mixed verbs (see page 57). Mixed verbs have the same stem in the perfect tense as in the imperfect. For example, the imperfect stem of the verb *bringen* (to bring) is *brach-*. To form the past participle of a mixed verb, you add **ge-** to the start of the imperfect stem and *-t* to the end. So the past participle of *bringen* is **ge**brach**t**. Here are the past participles of some other common mixed verbs:

brennen (to burn)	-	**ge**brann**t**
denken (to think)	-	**ge**dach**t**
kennen (to know)	-	**ge**kann**t**
wissen (to know)	-	**ge**wuss**t**

Past participles without *ge-*

Some verbs do not add **ge-** to the front when forming the past participle, mainly because it would make them very hard to pronounce. Verbs beginning with *be-*, *er-*, *ver-*, *emp-* or *ent-* don't add **ge-**, and neither do verbs ending in *-ieren*:

beginnen (to begin)	-	*begonnen*
besuchen (to visit)	-	*besucht*
erzählen (to tell)	-	*erzählt*
reparieren (to repair)	-	*repariert*
reservieren (to book)	-	*reserviert*

Fast facts

To form the past participle of a separable verb (e.g. *zumachen*) you put the **ge-** in between the prefix and the rest of the verb:

e.g. *Tanja hat das Fenster zu**ge**macht.*
(Tanja closed the window.)

Hast du dein neues Fahrrad mitgebracht?
Have you brought your new bicycle with you?

Ich habe es gestern gesehen. Es ist toll!
I saw it yesterday. It's great!

Danke. Ich habe es am Wochenende gekauft.
Thanks. I bought it at the weekend.

65

The Blumenkohl treasure: chapter 15

While they're waiting for lunch, the three friends read in the bald man's diary how he came across details of the Blumenkohl treasure...

Er hat es geschafft, die Kuckuck-Insel zu erreichen.

Am Eingang zu einer Höhle hat er eine rostige, alte Kiste gesehen.

Darin hat er einen Brief gefunden, der von einem Schatz sprach.

Ja, das war der Brief, den er gestohlen hat.

Zu Tisch! Hier kommt Vati.

Entschuldigung, ich habe eine sehr lange Sitzung gehabt.

New words

das Brot(-e)	bread
der Eingang(-̈e)	entrance
die Höhle(-n)	cave
die Kiste(-n)	chest (container)
das Mittagessen(-)	lunch
die Sitzung(-en)	meeting
der Tisch(-e)	table
das Zelt(-e)	tent
erklären	to explain
erreichen	to reach, to get to
finden*	to find
geben*	to give
legen	to put
mit'bringen	to bring with you
schaffen	to manage, to cope
sprechen*	to speak
stehlen*	to steal
suchen	to look for
vergessen*	to forget
warten auf	to wait for
darin	inside it
das macht nichts	it doesn't matter
Entschuldigung	sorry
fast	nearly
fertig	ready
gleich	immediately, in a minute
lang	long
rostig	rusty
Vati	Dad

67

The perfect tense with *sein*

Some verbs use *sein*, rather than *haben*, to form the perfect tense, for example *Ich bin gegangen* (I went). You have to learn which verbs use *sein*. Most of them are strong verbs, but there are some weak ones as well.

Strong verbs with *sein*

The verbs that use *sein* mostly refer either to a **change of place** (going, coming, arriving, etc.) or a **change of state** (dying, waking up, etc.).

Here are some common strong verbs which use *sein* (the past participles are given in brackets):

aufstehen (aufgestanden)	to get up
bleiben (geblieben)	to stay
fahren (gefahren)	to go, to drive
fallen (gefallen)	to fall
fliegen (geflogen)	to fly
gehen (gegangen)	to go, to walk
kommen (gekommen)	to come
laufen (gelaufen)	to run
schwimmen (geschwommen)	to swim
springen (gesprungen)	to jump
steigen (gestiegen)	to climb
sterben (gestorben)	to die
wachsen (gewachsen)	to grow

Werden and *sein*

Two other important verbs use *sein* in the perfect tense. These are *werden* (to become) and *sein* itself. So "I became ill" is *ich bin krank geworden* and "I have been ill" is *ich bin krank gewesen*.

Weak verbs

A few weak verbs also form the perfect tense with *sein*. These are shown here:

aufwachen (aufgewacht)	to wake up
begegnen (begegnet)	to meet
folgen (gefolgt)	to follow
klettern (geklettert)	to climb
passieren (passiert)	to happen
stürzen (gestürzt)	to fall, to plunge

e.g. *Wir **sind** früh aufgewacht.*
(We woke up early.)
*Was **ist** passiert?*
(What's happened?)

Ich bin hier drei Nächte geblieben. I stayed here three nights.

 Vorsicht!

Watch out for separable verbs. If their basic verb uses *sein* in the perfect tense, then they will use *sein* too:
e.g. *Ich bin heute angekommen.*
(I arrived today.)

Learning verbs

With each new strong verb you learn, try to remember the infinitive, plus the *er* forms of the present, imperfect and perfect tenses. For the verb "to go", you would learn:

gehen, geht, ging, ist gegangen.

You'll find a list of verbs set out like this on pages 114-115.

Fast facts

Some English verbs follow a very similar pattern to German verbs:

e.g. *singen, sang, hat gesungen*
(to sing, sang, has sung)

trinken, trank, hat getrunken
(to drink, drank, has drunk)

Perfect word order

In simple German sentences, the past participle goes at the end of a clause:
e.g. *Ich bin ins Kino **gegangen**.*
(I went to the cinema.)

If you start a sentence with a word like "yesterday", then the verb *haben* or *sein* must come next:
e.g. *Gestern **bin** ich ins Kino gegangen.*
(Yesterday, I went to the cinema.)

If you use a word like *weil* (because) or *dass* (that), then the verb *haben* or *sein* goes right to the end of the clause, after the past participle:
e.g. *Ich hoffe, dass Mutti mein Geschenk gekauft **hat**.*
(I hope that Mum has bought my present.)

Wilhelm ist heute Morgen spät aufgewacht.
Wilhelm woke up late this morning.

Er ist schnell aufgestanden und ist gleich in die Schule gegangen...
He got up quickly and went straight to school...

...aber er ist doch zu spät gekommen.
...but he still arrived late.

Und leider ist er der Lehrer!
And unfortunately, he's the teacher!

The Blumenkohl treasure: chapter 16

After lunch, Erich, Tanja and Monika go to the farm where the crook, Stefan Speck, is staying. When they arrive, they overhear a conversation that will take them to the next clue...

> Wir müssen zum Dreieich-Bauernhof gehen...

> ...um den Mann mit der Glatze und den Hinweis aus der Schule zu suchen.

> Kaffee, Herr Speck?

> Danke schön... Äh, ich wollte Sie etwas fragen.

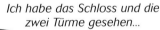

> Heute Morgen bin ich nach Turmstadt gefahren.

> Ich habe das Schloss und die zwei Türme gesehen...

> ...aber den zerstörten Turm habe ich nicht gefunden.

> Warum wollen Sie den sehen? Es sind nur alte Steine.

> Äh...ich mag Ruinen.

Na, sind Sie in den Park gegangen?

Ja, aber ich habe dort nichts gesehen.

Aha, Sie sind nicht bis zum Fluss hinuntergegangen.

Hallo Elke, wie geht's?

...Ja, der alte Turm ist am Fluss.

Ach, wirklich? Das ist sehr interessant.

Der nächste Hinweis muss im alten Turm sein.

New words

der Kaffee(-s)	coffee
die Ruine(-n)	ruin
der Stein(-e)	stone
fragen	to ask
hinunter'gehen*	to go down
etwas	something
heute Morgen	this morning
nur	only
wie geht's?	how are you?
wirklich	really
zerstört	destroyed, ruined

71

Using the perfect and possessives

The German perfect tense has two different meanings in English. For example, *er hat gestohlen* can mean "he has stolen" and "he stole". G*estohlen* and "stolen" are both past participles and they can both be used as adjectives to describe a noun, e.g. *gestohlene Papiere* (stolen papers).

Making adjectives

In German, you can use a past participle exactly as you would use an adjective. If you put the past participle before the noun, you have to add the correct endings:
e.g. *Das Geschäft ist geschlossen.*
(The shop is closed.)
Ich habe den versteckten Hinweis gefunden.
(I've found the hidden clue.)

Several actions

When the subject of a sentence does more than one action in the perfect tense, you don't have to repeat *haben* or *sein*. So "I ate an ice-cream and drank lemonade" becomes *Ich habe ein Eis gegessen und eine Limo getrunken.*

Gestern Abend... Yesterday evening...

habe ich meine Schwester angerufen,...
I phoned my sister,...

einen Brief geschrieben...
wrote a letter...

und mein Abendessen gegessen.
and ate my dinner.

This and that

The German word for "this" is *dieser*. Here, you can see the different endings it uses in the nominative, accusative, genitive and dative cases:

[m]	[f]	[n]	[pl]
dieser	diese	dieses	diese
diesen	diese	dieses	diese
dieses	dieser	dieses	dieser
diesem	dieser	diesem	diesen

The German for "that" is *jener*. It adds exactly the same endings as *dieser*. However, in everyday speech, you normally just use *der/die/das/die* plus the word *da*:
e.g. **Dieser** Rock ist schön, aber **der da** ist scheußlich. (This skirt is nice, but that one is horrible.)

Mine, yours, his, hers, etc.

In German, there are two ways to say that something is "mine", "yours, "theirs", etc. You can use the verb *gehören* (to belong to), followed by the dative case:

e.g. *Es gehört mir.*
(It belongs to me./It's mine.)
Der Papagei gehört ihm.
(The parrot belongs to him./The parrot's his.)

Another way to say who something belongs to is to use a special set of words, called **possessive pronouns** (see the box on the right). These add different endings to match the gender of the noun they are replacing. So, if you are talking about something feminine, e.g. *eine Tasche* (a bag), you say *Meine ist blau* (Mine is blue). If you are talking about something masculine, e.g. *ein Hund* (a dog), you say *Meiner ist schwarz* (Mine is black).

Possessive pronouns

[m]	[f]	
meiner	*meine*	mine
deiner	*deine*	yours
seiner	*seine*	his/its
ihrer	*ihre*	hers/its
uns(e)rer	*uns(e)re*	ours
eu(e)rer	*eu(e)re*	yours
ihrer	*ihre*	theirs
Ihrer	*Ihre*	yours

[n]	[pl]	
mein(e)s	*meine*	mine
dein(e)s	*deine*	yours
sein(e)s	*seine*	his/its
ihr(e)s	*ihre*	hers/its
unser(e)s	*uns(e)re*	ours
euer(e)s	*eu(e)re*	yours
ihr(e)s	*ihre*	theirs
Ihr(e)s	*Ihre*	yours

The letters shown in brackets are often left out.

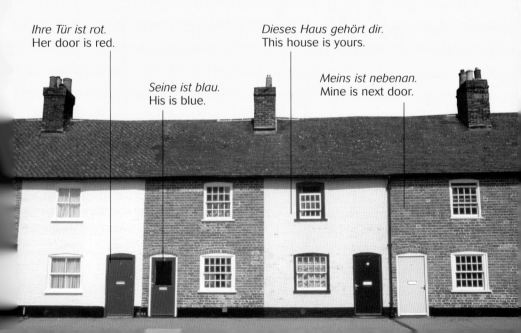

Ihre Tür ist rot.
Her door is red.

Dieses Haus gehört dir.
This house is yours.

Seine ist blau.
His is blue.

Meins ist nebenan.
Mine is next door.

The Blumenkohl treasure: chapter 17

Erich, Tanja and Monika go home to get their bikes and rush to the old tower to find the next clue before Stefan gets there. It takes them quite a while to find it...

Soon they are at the tower ruins.

Nichts! Ich hab' überall gesucht und jeden Stein untersucht.

Mensch! Ich hab' hier etwas gefunden.

Schaut! Das ist Tobias Blumenkohls Zeichen!

The three friends have found Tobias Blumenkohl's sign on an old plaque.

Wir haben diesen alten Turm als Denkmal für die Einwohner von Turmstadt erhalten.

Vor drei Jahren haben ihn die Piraten von der Pirateninsel zerstört, aber jetzt haben wir uns gerächt. Wir haben nun unseren letzten Kampf gegen sie gewonnen. Wir haben sie aus ihrer Festung auf der Insel vertrieben, und sie sind aus unserem Land verschwunden.

New words

das Denkmal(-ˉer)	monument
die Festung(-en)	fort, fortress
der Kampf(-ˉe)	battle, struggle
das Land(-ˉer)	country, land
der Pirat(-en)	pirate
der Zaun(-ˉe)	fence
entziffern	to decipher
erforschen	to explore
erhalten*	to preserve
gewinnen*	to win
sich rächen	to get your revenge
schicken	to send
untersuchen	to examine
verschwinden*	to disappear
vertreiben*	to expel
zerstören	to destroy
als	as (a)
dahin	(to) there
noch nicht	not yet
sofort	right away
wegen [+ genitive or dative]	because of

Note: After a modal verb such as *müssen,* you often leave out the infinitive verb if it is a verb of movement, e.g. *Wir müssen dahin.* (We have to go there.)

The words on the plaque give them a good idea of where they must go next. Translate it and see what you think...

The future tense

In English, to talk about future events, you normally use the future tense, e.g. "I will sing"/"I will be singing", or you can use "going to" plus a verb, e.g. "I'm going to sing". German also has a future tense, though it is less common than the English future tense. You can often just use the present tense instead.

Making the future tense

It's easy to form the German future tense. You take the present tense of the irregular verb *werden* and add the infinitive of the verb you are using. Here's the future tense of the verb *singen* (to sing):

Singen (future tense)

ich werde singen	I will sing
du wirst singen	you will sing
er/sie/es wird singen	he/she/it will sing
wir werden singen	we will sing
ihr werdet singen	you will sing
sie werden singen	they will sing
Sie werden singen	you will sing

Am Sonntag werde ich dir dein Geschenk geben, Vati. I'll give you your present on Sunday, Dad.

More about *werden*

When *werden* is used on its own, it means "to become", e.g. *Ich werde müde.* (I'm becoming/getting tired.) Don't confuse it with the verb *bekommen* (to receive, to get)!

Future tense word order

When you use the future tense, the present tense of *werden* comes second in the sentence, and the infinitive of the other verb goes to the end of the sentence:

e.g. *Ich **werde** am Sonntag in der Kirche **singen**.*
(I will sing in church on Sunday.)

*Nächstes Jahr **wird** meine Schwester an die Uni **gehen**.*
(Next year, my sister will be going to university.)

When you use a modal verb in the future tense along with another verb in the infinitive, the modal infinitive goes last:

e.g. *Ich **werde** am Sonntag in der Kirche **singen können**.*
(I will be able to sing in church on Sunday.)

Learning tip

Remember that *ich will kommen* means "I **want** to come". *Will* is part of the modal verb *wollen* (to want). The German for "I will come" is *ich werde kommen*.

Using the present

Sometimes both German and English use the present tense when talking about future events:
e.g. *Er kommt morgen früh.*
(He's coming tomorrow morning.)
But in German, you can often use the present tense, where in English you would use the future:
e.g. *Ich bin bald zurück.*
(I'll be back soon.)

Morgen fahre ich in Urlaub!
I'm going on holiday tomorrow!

Zu + infinitive

In German, if you use a main verb followed by an infinitive verb, you have to add the word *zu* (to) before the infinitive, e.g. *Er begann **zu** singen*. (He started to sing.)

The exceptions to this rule are the modal verbs and *gehen*:
e.g. *Ich muss wissen.* (I must know.)
Ich gehe schwimmen.
(I'm going swimming.)

⚡ Fast facts

If you use *zu* with the infinitive of a separable verb, *zu* goes between the prefix and the main part of the verb:

e.g. *Ich hoffe bald an**zu**kommen.*
(I hope to arrive soon.)
*Ich habe vor, dich ein**zu**laden.*
(I'm planning to invite you.)

Dieter fliegt morgen nach Nordamerika. Er wird zwei Wochen in den Bergen wandern.
Dieter is flying to North America tomorrow. He'll be hiking in the mountains for two weeks.

Er versucht einen guten Weg durch die Berge zu finden.
He's trying to find a good route through the mountains.

The Blumenkohl treasure: chapter 18

Erich, Tanja and Monika need to go to the fort on Pirates' island, but it's too late to go that night. Just in case Stefan finds the clue and gets ahead of them, they devise a very crafty way of throwing him off the scent...

> Also, wir müssen zur Pirateninsel fahren.

> Aber hier wird der Mann den Hinweis finden und...

> Wir werden doch zu spät ankommen. Heute geht's nicht.

> ...er wird vielleicht während der Nacht zur Insel fahren.

> Also, dann müssen wir diesen Hinweis mit Laub verdecken. So!

> Wir können auch eine falsche Spur hinterlassen.

> Großartig! Er wird in die falsche Richtung gehen und uns nicht stören.

> Na gut, wir müssen ihm einen Zettel dalassen.

> Ich habe eine gute Idee.

> Aber wo werden wir ihn verstecken?

A few minutes later...

Wir können ihn hier verstecken und sein Zeichen darauf setzen.

Erich und ich können ein gutes Versteck suchen.

Das ist wirklich großartig! Darauf wird er bestimmt hereinfallen.

Monika writes a note to confuse the crook and put him on a false trail.

B.T. lhow beL. nednif negömreV niem
dnu nelewuJ eniem alla ud tsriw troD.
nehes dnaW etedielkrev nettalpzloH tim
enie ud tsriw nennirD. nehegnienih ud
tsriw esieW eseid fuA. nehes rettiG enho
retsneF nie ud tsriw troD. nessüm neheg
nevabretlA ni ehcawieziloP ruz tsriw uD.
nies gireiwhcs driw eiS. ebagfuA etztel
enied tsi reiH. ebah nessalretnih hci eid,
nednufeg esiewniH ella ud tsah nun,
nhoS rebeil nieM.

New words

die Aufgabe(-n)	task
das Gitter(-)	grid, bars
das Juwel(-en)	jewel
das Laub [no plural]	leaves, foliage
die Nacht(-̈e)	night
die Richtung(-en)	direction
die Spur(-en)	trail, track
das Vermögen(-)	fortune
das Versteck(-e)	hiding-place
der Zettel(-)	note
da'lassen*	to leave here/there
herein'fallen* auf	to fall for
hinein'gehen*	to go, to come in
hinterlassen*	to leave behind
setzen	to put
stören	to bother, to disturb
verdecken	to cover, to hide
verstecken	to hide
auf diese Weise	(in) this way
bestimmt	definitely
drinnen	inside
falsch	wrong, false
großartig	wonderful, great
mit Holzplatten verkleidet	with wooden panels
ohne [+ accusative]	without
während [+ genitive]	during

Can you read Monika's writing and find out where she is sending Stefan the crook?

79

The Blumenkohl treasure: chapter 19

That evening, the policeman who didn't believe the three friends' story stumbles across Stefan Speck's picture in the wanted files. Then he lands a catch he hadn't been anticipating...

Meanwhile, outside the police station...

Ich gehe zuerst essen und, wenn es wirklich dunkel ist, komme ich zurück.

Sometime later…

Ah, endlich...

Nummer 7454
Stefan Speck
41 Jahre alt

Wegen leichten Diebstahls gesucht

Belohnung

Also, morgen gehe ich zum Blumenkohl-Haus.

Die Kinder werden mir vielleicht helfen können, ihn zu finden.

Then suddenly…

Er ist's! Äh... Halt! Sie sind verhaftet.

Oh! Was war denn das?

81

Making comparisons

Comparisons are when you say things like "taller", "tallest", "more important" or "the most important". You can make comparisons with adjectives, e.g. "a longer skirt", or with adverbs, e.g. "He runs fastest". "Taller", "longer" and "more important" are known as **comparatives**. "Tallest", "fastest" and "the most important" are known as **superlatives**.

Comparisons with adjectives

In German, to form the comparative of an adjective, you add -*er*, just as you do in English. So the German for "Annie is smaller" is *Annie ist kleiner*. Some short adjectives, such as *groß*, also add an umlaut (¨).

Sie sind größer.
They are taller.

Sie ist kleiner.
She is smaller.

Remember that if the adjective comes before the noun it describes, you need to add the correct adjective endings, e.g. *ein kleineres Haus* (a smaller house).

To form the superlative of a German adjective, you use *der/die/das* + adjective + -*st*, then add the appropriate endings: e.g. *Annie ist das kleinste Kind.* (Annie is the smallest child.)

Adjectives such as *groß* also add an umlaut (¨) in the superlative, e.g. *das größte Haus* (the biggest house). You can see a list of these adjectives in the "Fast facts" box.

Comparisons with adverbs

In German, to form the comparative of an adverb, you simply add -*er*: e.g. *Er läuft schneller.* (He runs faster.)

To form the superlative, you put *am* in front of the adverb and add -*sten* on the end of it: e.g. *Er läuft am schnellsten.* (He runs fastest.)

As with adjectives, some adverbs add an umlaut (¨) when they are used in comparisons (see the "Fast facts" box below).

Adjectives without noun

You can also use *am* + -*sten* with adjectives, when they are not followed by a noun:

e.g. *Er ist am größten.* (He is the tallest.)
Sie ist am kleinsten. (She is the smallest.)

Fast facts

These words all add an umlaut (¨) when used in comparisons: *alt* (old), *jung* (young), *schwach* (weak), *stark* (strong), *lang* (long), *kurz* (short), *klug* (clever), *dumm* (stupid), *warm* (warm), *kalt* (cold), *arm* (poor), *groß* (big), *hart* (hard), *scharf* (sharp), *krank* (ill).

Some exceptions

A few German adjectives and adverbs have irregular forms when used in comparisons:

Adjectives

gut	*besser*	*der beste*
(good)	(better)	(the best)
hoch	*höher*	*der höchste*
(high)	(higher)	(the highest)
nah	*näher*	*der nächste*
(near)	(nearer)	(the nearest)
viel	*mehr*	*der meiste*
(much)	(more)	(the most)

Adverbs

bald	*eher*	*am ehesten*
(soon)	(sooner)	(the soonest)
gern	*lieber*	*am liebsten*
(gladly)	(more gladly)	(the most gladly)
gut	*besser*	*am besten*
(well)	(better)	(the best)
viel	*mehr*	*am meisten*
(much)	(more)	(the most)

Older than, younger than

In English, you use the word "than" to link the two things you are comparing (e.g. Peter is older than Paul, the cat is younger than the dog, etc.). In German, you use *als*:

e.g. *Er ist älter **als** seine Schwester.*
(He's older **than** his sister.)
*Sie ist jünger **als** ihr Bruder.*
(She is younger **than** her brother.)

Just as...as

To compare things that are similar, English uses "(just) as...as" and German uses *(genau)so...wie*:
e.g. *Sein Freund ist **genauso** dumm **wie** er.*
(His friend is **just as** stupid **as** he is.)

You can also use *genauso* on its own with an adjective:
e.g. *Sie ist **genauso** groß.*
(She's **just as** tall.)

Die höchsten Segel sind auch am kleinsten.
The highest sails are also the smallest ones.

Dieses Boot ist viel größer als die anderen.
This boat is much bigger than the others.

Dieses Boot ist näher.
This boat is nearer.

Das da ist weiter entfernt.
That one is further away.

The next morning, the three friends borrow Ralf's boat to cross to Pirates' island. They get inside the ruined fort, but can they find the treasure and get out again?

Komisch. Das Tor ist normalerweise zu.

Ich gehe lieber nicht hinunter.

Ach, Mensch!

Schaut mal, es gibt vier Tunnel.

Oh, nein!

Kommt hierher! Schaut euch das mal an!

Wir können nicht mehr hinaus!

TUNNELS AM ENDE DES LÄNGSTEN

The three friends must go to the end of the longest tunnel. They measure the tunnels using footsteps. Erich and Monika each take one and Tanja does the other two.

New words

das Handtuch(-¨er)	towel, cloth
der Kerker(-)	dungeon
das Ruder(-)	oar
das Tor(-e)	gate
sich drehen	to go around
leihen*	to lend, to hire
sich (etwas) leihen*	to borrow (something)
rudern	to row
am Ende [+ genitive]	at the end (of)
(da) hinunter	down (there)
der/die/das andere	the other
einfach	simply, just
im Kreis	in circles
komisch	funny, strange
kräftig	strong, powerful
nass	wet

Mein Tunnel ist nicht so lang wie deiner.

Mein erster Tunnel war genauso lang wie deiner, aber mein zweiter Tunnel ist kürzer.

Meiner ist länger als Tanjas erster Tunnel.

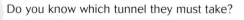

Do you know which tunnel they must take?

Conditional sentences

A conditional action is one that depends on something else happening, for example, "I **would buy** a new CD player, if I could afford it". This "would" form of the verb is known as the conditional. In German, to talk about conditional actions, you can either use the conditional or you can use another form of the verb, called the subjunctive. In English, the subjunctive is really only used in the phrase "If I **were** you..."

Making the conditional

To make the conditional in German, you use a special form of the verb *werden*, plus the infinitive of the verb you want. The infinitive goes to the end of the clause. Here you can see the conditional of the verb *gehen* (to go):

> *Gehen* (conditional)
>
> | | |
> |---|---|
> | *ich würde gehen* | I would go |
> | *du würdest gehen* | you would go |
> | *er/sie/es würde gehen* | he/she/it would go |
> | *wir würden gehen* | we would go |
> | *ihr würdet gehen* | you would go |
> | *sie würden gehen* | they would go |
> | *Sie würden gehen* | you would go |
>
> e.g. *Ich würde in die Stadt gehen, aber ich habe keine Zeit.* (I would go into town, but I don't have time.)

Sein, haben and modals

With *sein, haben* and modal verbs, it's more common to use the subjunctive instead of the conditional. To make the subjunctive of *haben* and modal verbs, you take the imperfect tense (see pages 56-57) and add an umlaut (¨), e.g. *ich hätte* (I would have) and *ich könnte* (I would be able/I could). The verbs *sollen* and *wollen* do not add an umlaut, e.g. *ich sollte* (I ought).

Sein goes like this: *ich wäre, du wärst, er/sie/es wäre, wir wären, ihr wäret, sie wären, Sie wären.*

If this happened, I would...

To say what you **would** do, if something else happened, you use the German word *wenn* (if) plus the conditional or the subjunctive. In everyday speech, you use the subjunctive with *sein, haben* and modal verbs, and the conditional with most other verbs, e.g. *Wenn ich viel Geld* **hätte**, **würde** *ich ein größeres Haus* **kaufen**. (If I **had** lots of money, I**'d buy** a bigger house.)

Ich würde dieses Haus kaufen, aber ich habe kein Geld.
I would buy this house, but I don't have any money.

> ## Fast facts
>
> | If this happened... | I would... |
> |---|---|
> | *wenn* + conditional or subjunctive | conditional or subjunctive |

If this happens, I will...

To say that you **will** do something, if something else happens, in German you can either use the present tense, or the present tense plus the future tense:

e.g. *Wenn ich Zeit* **habe**, **fahre** *ich in die Stadt.*
OR *Wenn ich Zeit* **habe**, **werde** *ich in die Stadt* **fahren**.
(If I **have** time, I**'ll go** into town.)

Wenn ich das alles esse, werde ich mich übergeben!
If I eat all this, I'll be sick!

Fast facts

If this happens...	I will...
wenn + present tense	present or future tense

Word order

After *wenn*, the verb always goes to the end of the clause. In the next part of the sentence, you have to turn the subject and verb around, so the verb comes first:

e.g. *Wenn ich einen Bruder* **hätte**, **würde** *ich mit ihm Fußball spielen.*
(If I **had** a brother, I **would** play football with him.)

Being polite

The "would" form of the verb is also often used in polite conversation. The polite way to ask for something is to say *ich möchte* (I would like, from the modal verb *mögen*) or *ich hätte gern* (I would like to have).

Was würdest du machen, wenn du einen versteckten Schatz finden würdest?
What would you do if you found some hidden treasure?

Ich würde eine Seereise machen.
I would go on a cruise.

Ich würde in den Weltraum fahren.
I would travel into space.

The Blumenkohl treasure: chapter 21

The three friends select the longest tunnel. Now, if there's any treasure to be found, surely they must be close...

Meanwhile, the policeman has gone to the Blumenkohl house...

Guten Tag, ich möchte mit Monika, Erich und Tanja sprechen.

New words

die Geschichte(-n)	story, history
die Mauer(-n)	wall
der Ring(-e)	ring
die Taschen- lampe(-n)	torch, flashlight
der Verbrecher(-)	criminal
danken [+ dative]	to thank
enden	to end
reichen	to pass
schnappen	to catch, to nab
sprechen* mit [+ dative]	to talk to
stören	to disturb
warten auf [+ acc]	to wait for
ziehen* an [+ dative]	to pull, to give...a pull
eisern	iron
ganz	whole
wenn	if
vielleicht	maybe, perhaps
zuerst	first of all

Ich möchte ihnen danken. Sie haben mir geholfen, einen Verbrecher zu schnappen!

Möchten Sie auf sie warten?

Nein, ich werde zurückkommen. Ich möchte Sie nicht stören.

Aber zuerst könnten Sie uns vielleicht die ganze Geschichte erzählen. Wir wissen nichts!

Writing a letter in German

There are two main types of letter: informal (for friends and family) and formal (for companies and people you don't know). Here are some basic guidelines for writing letters in German.

Structure

Every letter has a basic structure. When you're writing a letter in German, you normally put the name of your town or village in the top right-hand corner, followed by the date. At the end, you sign off with an appropriate farewell.

The date

If the date is Tuesday 5th September, you can either write *Dienstag, den 5. September* or just *den 5. September*. The date is written in the accusative case and the number is always followed by a full stop. You'll find a list of the days and the months on page 94.

Bonn, den 25. Oktober

Liebe Ulrike,

Vielen Dank für deinen Brief. Wie geht's dir? Mir geht's sehr gut, denn ich habe zwei Karten für ein Konzert in Berlin gewonnen. Komm mit! Es würde Spaß machen, und du könntest bei mir übernachten.

Schreib mir bald mit deiner Antwort.

Viele liebe Grüße!
Verena

Informal letters

When writing to friends and family, or people you know quite well, you start with the German word *lieb* (dear). *Lieb* is an adjective, so you have to add the correct endings, e.g. *lieber Erich, liebe Monika*.

Du, Ihr or Sie?

If you are writing to a friend or relative, you use *du*. If you are writing to a group of friends or relatives, use *ihr*. If you are writing to an older person you don't know so well, remember to use *Sie*.

Useful phrases

• *Vielen Dank für...* (Thanks for...) e.g. *Vielen Dank für deinen Brief.* (Thanks for your letter.)
• *Ich habe mich gefreut, wieder von dir zu hören.* (It was good to hear from you again.)
• *Es tut mir Leid, dass ich so lange nicht geschrieben habe.* (I'm sorry I haven't written for so long.)
• *Bitte, grüße auch X von mir.* (Give my love to X.)
• *Schreib mir bald.* (Write to me soon.)

Signing off

Use *Viele Grüße* (best wishes) for people you know quite well. For close friends and family, use *Viele liebe Grüße von deinem/deiner* + your name (lots of love from...) If you're using *ihr*, write *Viele liebe Grüße von eurem/eurer...*

Signing off

The usual way to finish a formal letter to a firm or to someone you don't know is: *Mit freundlichen Grüßen*. The equivalent in English is "Yours sincerely" or "Yours faithfully". Then you just sign your name.

Formal letters

If you're writing to a firm, or to someone you've never met before, you must use the *Sie* form. You should begin a formal letter with *Sehr geehrt-* followed by the appropriate form of address:
• *Sehr geehrte Damen und Herren* (Dear Sirs)
• *Sehr geehrter Herr* (Dear Sir)
• *Sehr geehrte Frau* (Dear Madam)
If you know the person's title and name, you add it after *Frau* or *Herr*: e.g. *Sehr geehrter Herr Dr. Braun* (Dear Dr Braun)
Sehr geehrte Frau Professor Müller (Dear Professor Müller)

Useful phrases

• *Bitte schicken Sie mir nähere Informationen zu...* (Please send me details of...)
• *Ich wäre dankbar, wenn Sie... könnten.* (I would be grateful if you could...)
• *Ich möchte wissen, ob...* (I'd like to know whether...)
• *In der Anlage sende ich...* (I enclose...)
• *Ich möchte...reservieren.* (I would like to book...)
• *Ich danke Ihnen im Voraus für...* (Thank you in advance for...)

London, den 4. Februar

Sehr geehrter Herr,

Im kommenden Sommer fahre ich mit meiner Familie nach Deutschland, und wir haben vor, einige Tage im Schwarzwald zu verbringen. Ich wäre dankbar, wenn Sie mir nähere Informationen zur Gegend schicken könnten. Senden Sie mir bitte auch eine Liste von Campingplätzen. Ich danke Ihnen im Voraus für Ihre Mühe.

Mit freundlichen Grüßen,

Paul Smith

How do I start a letter to a tourist information office?

91

The Blumenkohl treasure: chapter 22

Back at the old fort, they've found the treasure, and now just have to find a way out since the entrance has been jammed by fallen rocks...

> Also... Wir sollten einen Ausgang suchen.

> Schaut mal! Licht!

> Vielleicht finden wir einen, wenn wir zur Treppe zurückgehen.

> Puh!

> Tanja, wenn du die großen Steine da vorschiebst, sieht niemand die Spalte.

> Jetzt kann ich Ralf neue Ruder kaufen.

And so the three friends make it home to a hero's welcome.

New words

der Anteil(-e)	share, portion
der Artikel(-)	article
der CD-Spieler(-)	CD player
der Dieb(-e)	thief
der Held(-en)	hero
der Kurier(-e)	courier
die Leute [plural]	people
das Licht(-er)	light
der Monat(-e)	month
die Spalte(-n)	crack
die Treppe(-n)	steps, staircase
die Weihnachts- ferien [plural]	Christmas holidays
einverstanden sein	to agree
fassen	to catch
gratulieren [+ dat]	to congratulate
stoßen* auf [+ acc]	to find (by chance)
verbringen	to spend (time)
vor'schieben*	to push...in front
bevor	before
bis bald	see you soon
dummerweise	stupidly
hoffentlich	hopefully
jung	young
spannend	exciting
versteckt	hidden
zufällig	by chance

Once Erich and Tanja are back home in Berlin, Monika sends them a letter and a cutting from the local newspaper...

Montag, den 2. September

Liebe Tanja, lieber Erich,

Hier ist der Artikel aus dem Kurier, der unsere Geschichte erzählt. Er ist großartig! Was macht ihr mit eurem Anteil an der Belohnung? Mit meinem werde ich mir einen CD-Spieler kaufen.
Wenn eure Mutter einverstanden ist, besuche ich euch während der Weihnachtsferien. Also hoffentlich bis bald!

Viele Grüße,

Monika

KURIER

Freitag,
den 30. August

Der Schatz der Familie Blumenkohl

Monika Blumenkohl mit ihren Freunden Erich und Tanja Müller und ihrem Hund, Hüpfer.

Stefan Speck, der Dieb von seltenen Vögeln, der den Blumenkohl-Schatz stehlen wollte.

Der Monat August ist für Monika Blumenkohl und ihre Freunde Erich und Tanja eine spannende Zeit gewesen. Sie haben einen Schatz gefunden und der Polizei geholfen, den Verbrecher Stefan Speck zu fassen.

Vor vielen Jahren starb Monikas Urgroßvater, Tobias, auf einer entlegenen Insel. Er hinterließ eine Kiste. Diese Kiste war neben dem Eingang zu einer Höhle versteckt. Vor einigen Monaten war Speck auf derselben Insel. Dort suchte er sehr seltene Papageien, die er stehlen wollte.

Zufällig stieß er auf die alte Kiste und fand einen Brief von Tobias darin. Dieser Brief war an Monikas Großvater, Georg. Er war der erste Hinweis in einer Schatzsuche und brachte Speck nach Turmstadt, wo er ihn dummerweise verlor. Erich und Tanja, die gerade ankamen, um einige Tage bei ihrer Freundin Monika zu verbringen, fanden ihn. Die drei jungen Leute schafften es, den Schatz (Gold), der in der alten Piratenfestung versteckt war, zu finden, bevor der Verbrecher es tun konnte. Sie haben auch der Polizei geholfen, Speck zu fassen. Die drei Helden haben auch eine Belohnung von 2 000 Euro von der Polizei bekommen. Wir gratulieren!

Numbers and other useful words

Zahlen (numbers)

0	null	18	achtzehn
1	eins	19	neunzehn
2	zwei	20	zwanzig
3	drei	21	einundzwanzig
4	vier	22	zweiundzwanzig
5	fünf	23	dreiundzwanzig
6	sechs	30	dreißig
7	sieben	31	einunddreißig
8	acht	32	zweiunddreißig
9	neun	33	dreiunddreißig
10	zehn	40	vierzig
11	elf	41	einundvierzig
12	zwölf	42	zweiundvierzig
13	dreizehn	50	fünfzig
14	vierzehn	60	sechzig
15	fünfzehn	70	siebzig
16	sechzehn	80	achtzig
17	siebzehn	90	neunzig

100	hundert
101	hunderteins
150	hundertfünfzig
200	zweihundert
201	zweihunderteins
300	dreihundert

1,000	tausend
1,100	tausendeinhundert
2,000	zweitausend
10,000	zehntausend
100,000	hunderttausend
1,000,000	eine Million
2,000,000	zwei Millionen
1,000,000,000	eine Milliarde

1st	1.	der/die/das erste
2nd	2.	der/die/das zweite
3rd	3.	der/die/das dritte
7th	7.	der/die/das siebte
8th	8.	der/die/das achte
20th	20.	der/die/das zwanzigste
31st	31.	der/die/das einunddreißigste

Tage (days)

Montag	Monday
Dienstag	Tuesday
Mittwoch	Wednesday
Donnerstag	Thursday
Freitag	Friday
Samstag	Saturday
Sonntag	Sunday

Monate (months)

Januar	January
Februar	February
März	March
April	April
Mai	May
Juni	June
Juli	July
August	August
September	September
Oktober	October
November	November
Dezember	December

Das Datum (the date)

Der Wievielte ist heute?	What's the date today?
(am) Montag	on Monday
montags	on Mondays
im August	in August
der erste April	the first of April
der dritte Januar	the third of January
Freitag, den 7. März	Friday, March 7

Jahre (years)

1990	neunzehnhundertneunzig
2000	zweitausend
2001	zweitausendeins
2002	zweitausendzwei
2010	zweitausendzehn

Die Jahreszeiten (the seasons)

Frühling	spring
Sommer	summer
Herbst	autumn
Winter	winter
im Sommer	in (the) summer

Das Wetter (the weather)

die Temperatur(-en)	temperature
die Wetter- *vorhersage(-n)*	weather forecast
Wie ist das Wetter?	What's the weather like?
Das Wetter ist *schön./Es ist schön.*	The weather's fine./It's fine.
Das Wetter ist *schlecht/* *Es ist schlecht.*	The weather's bad/ It's bad.
Es regnet.	It's raining.
Es ist heiß.	It's hot.
Es ist sonnig.	It's sunny.
Die Sonne scheint.	The sun's shining.
Es ist kalt.	It's cold.
Es schneit.	It's snowing.
der Blitz(-e)	(flash of) lightning
der Frost	frost
das Gewitter(-)	thunderstorm
der Hagel	hail
der Himmel	sky
der Regen	rain
der Schnee	snow
die Sonne	sun
die Wolke(-n)	cloud

Useful words

bis bald	see you soon
bis nachher/ *bis später*	see you later
bitte	please
danke (schön)	thank you, thanks
ja	yes
nein	no
guten Morgen	good morning
guten Abend	good evening
gute Nacht	good night
guten Tag	hello
hallo	hi
tschüs	bye
(auf) Wiedersehen	goodbye
(auf) Wiederhören	goodbye (on the phone)

Useful expressions

Wie sagt man das auf Deutsch?
(How do you say that in German?)
Was bedeutet dieses Wort?
(What does this word mean?)
Ich verstehe nicht.
(I don't understand.)
Ich weiß nicht.
(I don't know.)
Es tut mir Leid./Entschuldigung.
(I'm sorry.)
Bitte schön.
(You're welcome.)

Declensions and dialects

Nouns and pronouns are used in different cases depending on the job they are doing in the sentence. You can tell the case of a noun by looking at the words that go with it (such as the words for "the" and "a"). When a word is written in a table with all its different forms, it is called a **declension**.

The four cases

- **Nominative** - when the noun or pronoun is the subject of the sentence.
- **Accusative** - when the noun or pronoun is the direct object, or when it follows one of a group of prepositions.
- **Genitive** - when the noun or pronoun is the owner of something.
- **Dative** - when the noun or pronoun is the indirect object, or when it follows one of a group of prepositions.

The words for "the":

	m	f	n	pl
nom	der	die	das	die
acc	den	die	das	die
gen	des	der	des	der
dat	dem	der	dem	den

The words for "a":

	m	f	n
nom	ein	eine	ein
acc	einen	eine	ein
gen	eines	einer	eines
dat	einem	einer	einem

Adjectives

In German, adjectives used **before** a noun (e.g. "the **small** tent") change to match the gender and case of the noun. Adjectives add different endings, depending on whether they are used after the words for "the" or "a", or alone with a noun. See how the endings change with *rot* (red).

Adjectives used alone with a noun:

	m	f	n	pl
nom	roter Wein	rote Seife	rotes Papier	rote Äpfel
acc	roten Wein	rote Seife	rotes Papier	rote Äpfel
gen	roten Weins	roter Seife	roten Papiers	roter Äpfel
dat	rotem Wein	roter Seife	rotem Papier	roten Äpfeln

Adjectives used with the word for "the", plus a noun:

	m	f	n	pl
nom	der rote Pulli	die rote Tasche	das rote Auto	die roten Äpfel
acc	den roten Pulli	die rote Tasche	das rote Auto	die roten Äpfel
gen	des roten Pullis	der roten Tasche	des roten Autos	der roten Äpfel
dat	dem roten Pulli	der roten Tasche	dem roten Auto	den roten Äpfeln

Adjectives used with the word for "a", plus a noun:

	m	f	n
nom	ein roter Pulli	eine rote Tasche	ein rotes Auto
acc	einen roten Pulli	eine rote Tasche	ein rotes Auto
gen	eines roten Pullis	einer roten Tasche	eines roten Autos
dat	einem roten Pulli	einer roten Tasche	einem roten Auto

The German language is spoken by approximately one hundred million people worldwide. It is the national language of Germany and Austria, and is one of the four official languages in Switzerland. The standard form of German is known as *Hochdeutsch* ("high German"), but people in different areas may speak slightly different forms, known as **dialects**. Don't be put off if you find a dialect hard to understand at first.

Language families

English and German are both West Germanic languages, which means they are descended from the same branch of a language family tree. That's why English and German have many words in common, e.g. *blind, warm, Butter, Finger, Hand, Name, Ring* and *Winter*.

Language borrowing

Sometimes the English language "borrows" German words, such as "kindergarten" and "muesli". More recently, the German language has borrowed many English words, in particular words relating to modern life, e.g. *der Computer, die E-Mail, die Website, die Compactdisc, das Mountainbike* and *das Make-up*.

False friends

There are some words that look identical in both German and English, but mean very different things. These are known as "false friends" and can be very misleading. For instance, the German word *bald* means "soon" and the word *fast* means "almost". More dangerous could be the misinterpretation of the German word *Gift* which means poison! The German word for "gift" is *Geschenk*.

German expressions

Every language has its own special phrases, or idioms, such as the English expression "It's raining cats and dogs". In German, there are many idioms that add colour to the language. Here are some examples:

There are a few German idioms that use broken bone imagery. To say "It could be worse", you literally say "That's not a broken leg" (*Das ist kein Beinbruch*). And one way of wishing someone "Good luck!" is *Hals- und Beinbruch!* which literally translates as "broken neck and leg".

In German, there's an idiom that stems from playing cards. You can say *alles auf eine Karte setzen* (to put everything on one card), meaning that you pin all your hopes on one thing. The English equivalent is "put all your eggs in one basket".

In English, prudent people advise you not to throw money down the drain. In German, the advice is "not to throw money out of the window" (*das Geld nicht zum Fenster hinauswerfen*).

And if someone accuses you of sitting there like a question mark (*dasitzen wie ein Fragezeichen*), they mean you are slouching.

German pronunciation guide

Pronunciation is how words sound. In German, many letters are not pronounced in the same way as in English. German also has groups of letters that are said in a special way.

The list below tells you roughly how letters and groups of letters are usually pronounced. Letters missing from the list sound the same, or nearly the same, as in English. Bear in mind, though, that people say things differently depending on where they come from.

Many of the sounds used in German do not have an exact English equivalent. So, if you can, ask a German speaker to make the sounds and say the example words given here, so that you can copy what you hear.

Vowels

In German, vowel sounds can be long or short. Often, if a vowel comes before a single consonant, it is long, and if it comes before two consonants, it is short. Double vowels are especially long, for example in *Paar, Meer* and *Boot*.

a (short) sounds like the "u" in "cut", with a hint of the "a" in "cat", for example in *danke*.
a (long) sounds like "a" in "arm", for example in *Vater*.

e (short) sounds like the "e" in "get", for example in *wenn*. It is always pronounced, even at the end of a word, for example in *Hose*.
e (long) sounds a bit like the "a" in "bathe", for example in *Weg*.

i (short) sounds like the "i" in "bit", for example in *ich*.
i (long) sounds like the "ee" in "see", for example in *Kilo*.

o (short) sounds like the "o" in "not", for example in *Sonne*.

o (long) sounds a bit like the "aw" in "crawl", for example in *Hose*.

u (short) sounds like the "u" in "put", for example in *Mutter*.
u (long) sounds like the "u" in "rule", for example in *Schuhe*.

Groups of vowels

ai and **ei** sound like the "i" in "mine", for example in *Kai* and *klein*.

au sounds a bit like the "ow" in "cow", for example in *Haus*.

eu sounds like the "oy" in "toy", for example in *heute*.

ie sounds like the "ee" in "feet", for example in *spielen*.

ä, äu, ö, ü, y

ä sounds a bit like the "a" in "care", for example in *spät*.

äu sounds like the "oy" in "toy", for example in *Häuser*.

ö sounds a bit like the "ea" in "earth", for example in *schön*.

ü is a sharp "u" sound, for example in *über*. Round your lips to say "oo", then try to say "ee" and you will be close to the right pronunciation.

y is said like **ü**, for example in *Typ*.

Consonants

b and **d** are usually pronounced the same as in English. However, when they come at the end of a word, **b** sounds like "p", for example in *Kalb*, and **d** sounds like "t", for example in *Hand*.

g is usually said like the "g" in "go", for example in *Geld*. However, if **g** comes after "i" at the end of a word, it is said like the "h" in "huge", for example in *fertig*.

h is usually said as in English, for example in *holen*. However, it is not normally sounded when it comes after a vowel, but it makes the vowel long, for example in *sehen*.

j sounds like the "y" in "yes", for example in *ja*.

r is a slightly growling "r" sound made at the back of the throat, for example in *rot*.

s sounds like "s" in "sea", for example in *Haus*. However, before a vowel, it sounds like "z" in "zoo", for example in *singen*.

ss and **ß** are the two ways that German has of writing "ss". They both sound the same (like an English "ss"). After a short vowel,

you use **ss**, for example in *muss*. After a long vowel, you use **ß**, for example in *größer*. You always use **ß** after two vowels that come together, for example in *heiß*.

The rules for when to use **ß** have changed recently, so you may still see words like *muß* in older books.

v is said like an English "f", as in "fine", for example in *Vater*.

w is said like an English "v". It sounds like "v" in "very", for example in *wenn*.

z sounds like the "ts" in "hits", for example in *zehn*.

Groups of consonants

ch sounds like the "h" in "huge", for example in *ich*. However, after "a", "o", "u" or "au", it sounds like the "ch" sound in the Scottish word "loch", for example in *lachen*.

chs usually sounds like the "x" in "axe", for example in *wachsen*.

ng sounds like the "ng" in "singer" (not like the "ng" in "finger"), for example in *singen*.

sch sounds like the "sh" in "shoe", for example in *Schule*.

sp and **st** at the start of a word have a "sh" sound before the "p" and the "t", for example in *spielen* or *Stadt*.

th sounds like an English "t" (not like an English "th"), for example in *Apotheke*.

Speech bubble key: chapters 1 to 5

Chapter 1
- *Erich, schau mal!* Erich, look!
- *Da ist die Küste!* There's the coast!
- *Ja, und da ist auch eine Stadt.* Yes, and there's a town too.
- *Es ist ein Hafen.* It's a port.
- *Ein Fluss!* A river!
- *Ein See!* A lake!
- *Ein Dorf!* A village!
- *Berge!* Mountains!
- *Schau! Dort drüben ist Turmstadt.* Look! That's Turmstadt over there.
- *Ja. Da sind die Brücken...* Yes. There are the bridges...
- *....und die beiden Türme.* ...and the two towers.
- *Oh, hier ist der Flughafen.* Oh, here's the airport.
- *Toll! Bonbons.* Great! Sweets.
- *Was ist das, Tanja?* What's that, Tanja?
- *Das ist die Karte.* It's the map.
- *Und hier ist das Blumenkohl-Haus.* And here's the Blumenkohl house.
- *Ja, da ist das Haus.* Yes, there's the house.

Chapter 2
- *Ich habe eine kleine schwarze Tasche.* I've got a small black bag.
- *He, Erich! Du hast auch ein Zelt.* Hey, Erich! You've got a tent as well.
- *Ach ja, ich habe ein grünes Zelt.* Oh yes, I've got a green tent.
- *Oh! Entschuldigung!* Oh! Sorry!
- *Er ist groß.* He's tall.
- *Ich bin müde...* I'm tired...
- *Ein grüner Koffer...eine blaue Tasche...* A green suitcase...a blue bag...
- *Ich habe eine grüne Tasche.* I've got a green bag.
- *Danke, Sie sind sehr nett.* Thank you. You are so kind.
- *Hallo, Monika? Hier spricht Tanja.* Hello Monika? It's Tanja.
- *Wir sind in Turmstadt...* We're in Turmstadt...
- *Nein, es geht. Wir haben deine Karte.* No, it's all right. We have your map.
- *Das ist deine Tasche.* This is your bag.
- *Aber nein, das ist seine Tasche.* No it's not, it's his bag.
- *Mein Rucksack ist rot.* My rucksack is red.
- *Mein Gepäck ist grau.* My luggage is grey.
- *Hier ist Ihr Koffer, Fräulein.* Here's your suitcase, Miss.

Chapter 3
- *Du gehst zu langsam.* You're walking too slowly.
- *Nein, ich genieße die Landschaft.* No I'm not, I'm enjoying the scenery.
- *Ach ja, die Sonne scheint...* Oh yes, the sun's shining...
- *...und die Vögel singen.* ...and the birds are singing.
- *Entschuldigung. Wir suchen den Campingplatz.* Excuse me, we're looking for the campsite.
- *Das ist leicht! Ihr fahrt geradeaus.* That's easy! You go straight ahead.
- *Ich will einen Tisch im Schatten.* I want a table in the shade.
- *Ich will eine eiskalte Limo.* I want an ice-cold lemonade.

- *Ich möchte eine Limo.* I'd like a lemonade.
- *Und ich möchte einen Orangensaft, bitte.* And I'd like an orange juice, please.
- *Zahlen, bitte!* The bill, please!
- *Hast du meinen Fotoapparat?* Have you got my camera?
- *Wir wollen Fahrräder leihen.* We want to hire some bikes.

The mysterious letter:
A desert island, 1893
My dear son Georg, I am an old man. I am all alone here, and my house near Turmstadt stands empty. I have a secret. I am very wealthy. You now get all my treasure. You'll find the first clue in the Blumenkohl house. You're looking for the two ships. Farewell, Tobias Blumenkohl

Chapter 4
- *Guten Tag. Wir sind Monikas Freunde.* Hello. We're Monika's friends.
- *Guten Tag. Ich bin ihre Mutter.* Hello. I'm her mother.
- *Ich heiße Heidrun...und hier ist unser Hund, Hüpfer.* My name's Heidrun...and this is our dog, Hüpfer.
- *Wem gehört diese Katze?* Who does this cat belong to?
- *Monika. Sie heißt Kratzer.* Monika. Her name's Kratzer.
- *Hier ist das Zimmer meiner Eltern...mein Zimmer und...das Zimmer von dem Untermieter.* Here's my parents' bedroom...my room and...the lodger's room.
- *Hier ist mein Lieblingszimmer.* Here's my favourite room.
- *Es ist das Atelier meiner Mutter.* It's my mother's studio.
- *Das ist ein altes Bild des Blumenkohl-Hauses.* That's an old picture of the Blumenkohl house.
- *Das ist ein Porträt von Monikas Großvater, Georg.* That's a portrait of Monika's grandfather, Georg.
- *Ach nein, es ist Fresser, die Ziege der Nachbarn!* Oh no, it's Fresser, the neighbours' goat!
- *Wem gehören diese Kleider?* Who do these clothes belong to?
- *Sie gehören meinem Bruder.* They belong to my brother.
- *Und dieses Fernglas?* And these binoculars?
- *Es gehört auch Erich.* They also belong to Erich.
- *Diese Brille ist toll.* These glasses are great.
- *Sie gehört Tanja.* They belong to Tanja.

Chapter 5
- *Warte! Langsam.* Wait! Go slowly.
- *Bleib ruhig, Fresser!* Keep still, Fresser!
- *Wirf das Seil!* Throw the rope!
- *Sei brav, Hüpfer!* Be good, Hüpfer!
- *Pass auf!* Watch out!
- *Zieht fest!* Pull hard!
- *Schließen Sie schnell das Tor!* Shut the gate quickly!
- *Beeilen Sie sich!* Hurry!
- *Ihr müsst alles anschauen - die alte Kirche, die Höhlen, Alterhaven...* You must look at everything - the old church, the caves, Alterhaven...

Chapters 5 to 9

- *...und ich muss in Alterhaven schnell einkaufen gehen.* ...and I must quickly do some shopping in Alterhaven.
- *Bis später.* See you later.
- *Man muss das Tor schließen.* You have to shut the gate.
- *Geh nach links...und nimm den ersten Weg rechts.* Turn left...and take the first path on the right.
- *Hüpfer, komm hierher!* Hüpfer, come here!
- *Das muss das Blumenkohl-Haus sein.* That must be the Blumenkohl house.
- *Ich muss diesen Hinweis schnell finden.* I must find this clue quickly.
- *Zuerst muss ich meine Nagelfeile finden.* First, I have to find my nail file.
- *Sei ruhig!* Be quiet!
- *Diese Schlösser müssen sehr alt sein.* These locks must be very old.

Chapter 6

- *Guten Tag, Frau Blumenkohl.* Hello, Mrs Blumenkohl.
- *Guten Tag.* Hello.
- *Haben Sie Äpfel?* Do you have any apples?
- *Haben Sie einen Korb?* Do you have a basket?
- *Ich möchte zwei Kilo Orangen.* I'd like two kilos of oranges.
- *Warum ist die Apotheke geschlossen?* Why is the pharmacy closed?
- *Frau Salbe ist krank.* Mrs Salbe is ill.
- *Entschuldigen Sie, wo ist die Bäckerei?* Excuse me, where is the bakery?
- *Was ist das?* What's that?
- *Das ist ein Krebs.* It's a crab.
- *Was kosten diese Kuchen?* How much do these cakes cost?
- *Wie viele Brötchen wollen Sie?* How many rolls do you want?
- *Was willst du?* What do you want?
- *Kann ich ein Eis haben?* Can I have an ice cream?
- *Was suchst du, Tanja?* What are you looking for, Tanja?
- *Wo ist er? Ah.* Where is it? Ah.
- *Monika, kannst du diesen Brief erklären?* Monika, can you explain this letter?
- *Soll das ein Witz sein?* Is it meant to be a joke?
- *Klasse! Das ist eine echte Schatzsuche!* Great! A real treasure hunt!

Chapter 7

- *Die Tür ist nicht abgeschlossen.* The door isn't locked.
- *Aber die Fahrräder sind nicht da.* But the bikes aren't there.
- *Sei ruhig, Hüpfer! Du darfst nicht so laut bellen!* Be quiet, Hüpfer! You mustn't bark so loudly!
- *Was suchst du?* What are you looking for?
- *Es ist niemand da.* There's no one there.
- *Da ist doch irgendwo ein Einbrecher!* But there's a burglar about somewhere!
- *Welche Schiffe? Es gibt hier keine Schiffe.* What ships? There aren't any ships here.
- *Guten Abend, Liebling. Guten Abend, Uli.* Good evening, darling. Good evening, Uli.
- *Guten Abend, Schätzchen... Ach nein! Ich finde keine Kopfschmerztabletten.* Good evening, darling... Oh no! There aren't any headache tablets.
- *Und weißt du warum? Die Apotheke ist geschlossen.* And do you know why? The pharmacy is closed.

- *Ich habe nichts, keine Tabletten, keine Pflaster...* I haven't got anything, no tablets, no plasters...
- *Hallo allerseits!* Hi, everyone!
- *Ach! Schaut bloß nicht herüber!* Oh! Just don't look over here!
- *Hier sind die zwei Schiffe.* Here are the two ships.
- *Oh, da draußen ist ein Mann.* Oh, there's a man outside.
- *Monika, wer ist dieser Mann?* Monika, who's that man?
- *Das weiß ich nicht.* I don't know.
- *Es ist nicht Uli, der Untermieter.* It's not Uli, the lodger.
- *Wo seid ihr? Das Essen ist fertig!* Where are you? The food's ready!
- *Okay. Wir kommen gleich.* OK. We're coming right away.
- *Schaut! Sie sind nicht ganz gleich!* Look! They're not exactly the same!

Chapter 8
- *Gehen wir einkaufen, Liebling.* Let's go shopping, darling.
- *Warte! Ich lese meine Zeitung.* Wait! I'm reading my newspaper.
- *Helgas Zug kommt bald an.* Helga's train is arriving soon.
- *Wann fangen die Prüfungen an?* When do the exams begin?
- *Fang schon an!* Go on, start.
- *Sie isst Käse.* She's having cheese.
- *Isst du Pommes frites?* Are you having chips?
- *Ja, ja, ich esse gern Pommes frites.* Oh yes, I like chips.
- *Gemüse esse ich nie.* I never eat vegetables.
- *Was machen diese doofen Kinder da? Sie stören sehr.* What are those stupid kids doing? They're really getting in the way.
- *Und überhaupt, warum machen sie Fotos?* And anyhow, why are they taking photos?
- *Pass auf! Er trägt eine große Schüssel Suppe herein!* Watch out! He's bringing in a big bowl of soup!
- *Also, jetzt reicht's! Hau ab!* Right, that's enough now! Clear off!
- *He! Wir gehen.* Hey! We're going.
- *Schaut mal! Ich habe den nächsten Hinweis...* Look! I've got the next clue...

Chapter 9
- *Schaut mal! Seht ihr den Mann mit der Glatze?* Look! Do you see the man with the bald head?
- *Beim Ausgang...neben der großen Frau in Rot.* Near the exit...next to the tall woman in red.
- *Es ist der Mann vom Flughafen!* It's the man from the airport.
- *Es ist der Mann mit dem Brief!* It's the man with the letter!
- *Es ist der Mann aus dem Garten!* It's the man from the garden!
- *Es ist derselbe Mann!* It's the same man!
- *Schnell! Er will unseren Schatz.* Quickly! He wants our treasure.
- *Oje! Der Mann mit der Glatze! Da...vor dem Brunnen.* Oh no! The bald man! There...in front of the fountain.
- *Er kommt auf den Kai.* He's coming onto the quay.
- *Schnell! Kommt hinter dieses Netz.* Quick! Come behind this net!
- *Es ist schon gut.* It's OK.
- *Also, leg den Zettel und die Fotos auf diese Bank.* Right, put the note and the

photos on this bench.
- *Hast du eine Lupe?* Have you got a magnifying glass?
- *Ja, aber zu Hause.* Yes, but at home.
- *Kommt, wir gehen zu meinem Kumpel, Ralf. Er wohnt gegenüber dem Bahnhof.* Come on, let's go to my mate Ralph's. He lives opposite the station.
- *Ja, ich habe eine Lupe... Sie ist auf meinem Tisch auf dem Speicher.* Yes, I've got a magnifying glass... It's on the table up in the attic.

The note:
The next clue is in a building in Alterhaven. Find the answers to these questions: Where is the dog? Where is the bench? Where is the cow? Where is the farm?

Chapter 10
- *Warum versteckt ihr euch?* Why are you hiding?
- *Wir gehen nicht gern in die Schule.* We don't like school.
- *Wie viel Uhr ist es?* What's the time?
- *Es ist acht Uhr, Frau Meyer.* It's eight o'clock, Mrs Meyer.
- *Und jetzt?* And now?
- *Es ist Viertel nach neun.* It's quarter past nine.
- *Kurt, um wie viel Uhr wäschst du dich vormittags?* Kurt, what time do you wash in the morning?
- *Um halb acht.* At half past seven.
- *Ziehst du dich ganz allein an?* Do you get dressed all on your own?
- *Ja, natürlich.* Yes, of course.
- *Ich fühle mich nicht sehr wohl.* I don't feel very well.
- *Also, beruhigt euch!* Right, calm down!
- *Schau! Das ist der Buntstift, der fehlt.* Look! That's the coloured pencil that's missing.
- *He! Das sind meine Bilder, die du zerreißt.* Hey! Those are my pictures you're tearing up.
- *Siehst du das alte Foto da?* Do you see that old photo?
- *Oh! Das muss der Hinweis sein, den wir suchen.* Oh! That must be the clue we're looking for.
- *Es ist Tobias Blumenkohl, der das Band durchschneidet.* That's Tobias Blumenkohl cutting the ribbon.
- *Und da ist das Zeichen, das sich auf allen seinen Hinweisen befindet.* And there's the sign that's on all his clues.
- *Wir können heute Abend zurückkommen.* We can come back this evening.
- *Gute Idee!* Good idea!

Chapter 11
- *Was tun Sie hier? Reparieren Sie das Fotokopiergerät?* What are you doing here? Are you mending the photocopier?
- *Äh, ja, das mache ich. Ich bin Mechaniker.* Er, yes, I am. I'm a mechanic.
- *Ja...ich verpacke eben ein kaputtes Teil.* Yes...I'm just wrapping up a broken part.
- *Also, geht's jetzt?* So it's OK now?
- *Äh, ja.* Er, yes.
- *Kann ich zumachen, Herr Streng?* Can I close up, Mr Streng?

- *Ja, natürlich.* Yes, of course.
- *Na, wie kommen wir hinein?* Now then, how do we get in?
- *Kommt schon!* Come on!
- *Was machst du, Tanja?* What are you doing, Tanja?
- *Sei nicht dumm... Ich suche das Foto...* Don't be stupid... I'm looking for the photo...
- *Zu spät! Der Mann mit der Glatze hat schon den Hinweis.* Too late! The bald man has already got the clue.
- *Woher weißt du das?* How do you know that?
- *Weil das da seine Aktentasche ist.* Because that's his briefcase.
- *Na schön, wir gehen zur Polizeiwache, um die Tasche abzugeben.* Right, we're going to the police station to hand in the case.
- *Sie ist zu.* It's closed.
- *Na gut, dann müssen wir morgen früh zurückkommen.* OK, then we'll have to come back tomorrow morning.
- *Kennst du den Kommissar?* Do you know the inspector?
- *Ja... Er ist ziemlich nett.* Yes... He's quite nice.

Chapter 12
- *Was machen wir mit der Aktentasche?* What do we do with the briefcase?
- *Zeigen wir sie deinen Eltern?* Do we show it to your parents?
- *Nein, wir dürfen sie ihnen nicht zeigen.* No, we mustn't show it to them.
- *Zuerst müssen wir der Polizei alles erzählen.* First, we have to tell the police everything.
- *Das Essen ist fertig!* Dinner's ready!
- *Ich kann sie in meinem Zelt verstecken.* I can hide it in my tent.
- *Gute Idee.* Good idea.
- *Der Mann mit der Glatze hat den Hinweis aus der Schule.* The bald man's got the clue from the school.
- *Um ihn zu finden, müssen wir den Mann mit der Glatze suchen.* To find it, we have to look for the bald man.
- *Seine Adresse ist vielleicht in seiner Aktentasche.* Maybe his address is in his briefcase.
- *Setz dich neben mich.* You sit next to me.
- *Tanja, reich ihr meine Taschenlampe.* Tanja, pass her my torch.
- *Ein Tagebuch, eine Zeitung...* A diary, a newspaper...
- *Aber schaut darunter... Da sind Papierschnitzel.* But look underneath... There are some bits of paper.
- *Es ist eine zerrissene Postkarte.* It's a torn up postcard.
- *Aber können wir sie noch lesen?* But can we still read it?

The postcard jigsaw:
Lieber Stefan, Vielen Dank für deinen Brief. Ja, Lothar und Anna Lauterback wohnen in der Nähe von Turmstadt. Du bittest mich um ihre Adresse. Hier ist sie: Dreieich Bauernhof, Brückenstraße, bei Alterhaven. Warum Turmstadt? Es ist nicht so interessant. Jedenfalls haben sie wahrscheinlich ein Zimmer frei für dich. Ich empfehle sie dir. Bei ihnen isst man gut, und es ist dort schön ruhig. Also, schöne Ferien! Natascha

Chapters 12 to 16

Dear Stefan, many thanks for your letter. Yes, Lothar and Anna Lauterback live near Turmstadt. You ask me for their address. Here it is: Dreieich Farm, Brückenstraße, near Alterhaven. Why Turmstadt? It's not so interesting. Anyhow, they probably have a room for you. I recommend them to you. You eat well at their place and it's lovely and quiet. So, have a nice holiday! Natascha

Chapter 13

- *Also, wo war diese Aktentasche?* So, where was this briefcase?
- *Sie war auf dem Kopiergerät in der Schule.* It was on the photocopier in the school.
- *Und warum wart ihr dort?* And why were you there?
- *Weil wir einen Schatz suchen.* Because we're looking for treasure...
- *Ja, und in der Schule war ein Hinweis.* Yes, and there was a clue in the school.
- *Welcher Schatz?* What treasure?
- *Er gehört meiner Familie.* It belongs to my family.
- *Ach so, ich verstehe. Und dieser Gauner will ihn stehlen.* Aha, I see. And this crook wants to steal it...
- *Genau! Der Hinweis ist ein altes Foto.* Exactly! The clue is an old photo.
- *Gestern Abend war das Foto nicht mehr da...* Last night the photo wasn't there any more...
- *...aber die Aktentasche vom Gauner war da.* ...but the crook's briefcase was there.
- *Sie gehört höchstwahrscheinlich dem Lehrer.* It's most probably the teacher's.
- *Aber nein, der Gauner hatte sie vorher.* But no, the crook had it before.
- *Das reicht! Geht jetzt nach Hause.* That's enough! Go home now.
- *Bringen Sie diese Aktentasche schnell zur Schule zurück.* Quickly take this briefcase back to the school.
- *Pech! Aber wir können ohne die Polizei weitermachen.* Too bad! But we can carry on without the police.
- *Glücklicherweise kennen wir die Adresse von dem Mann mit der Glatze.* Luckily we know the bald man's address.
- *Oh, schaut mal! Ich habe noch das Tagebuch, das in der Aktentasche war.* Oh look! I've still got the diary that was in the briefcase!
- *Es war in meiner Tasche.* It was in my pocket.

Chapter 14

- *Was ist das?* What's that?
- *Es war im Tagebuch.* It was in the diary.
- *Es sieht interessant aus...* It looks interesting...

The magazine cutting:

Rare birds of the Seltnafugal islands

A hundred years ago, there were lots of blue parrots on the Seltnafugal islands. The inhabitants worshipped them and built temples in their honour. You very rarely find these birds now and you are not allowed to catch them. Last year, you could see a few now and again on a remote desert island called Kuckuck.

The message:

Mr Speck, Get me a pair of blue parrots for my collection. Your fee: 15,000 euros. Mrs Eule

- *Mensch! Die Seltnafugal-Inseln... Mein Urgroßvater ging oft dahin, um die Pflanzen anzusehen.* Wow! The Seltnafugal islands... My great-grandfather often went there to look at the plants.
- *Er war Botaniker.* He was a botanist...
- *Und der Mann mit der Glatze war auf dieser Inselgruppe, um Papageien zu stehlen.* And the bald man was on those islands to steal some parrots.
- *Kommt schon! Ich will euch etwas zu Hause zeigen.* Come on, I want to show you something at home.

The letter:
Dear Sir, Sadly, your father is probably dead. He knew our islands well, but at the time of his disappearance, he was looking for plants on some dangerous and very remote islands. He was working with two colleagues. They had a good boat, but it was the stormy season. Pedro Peperoni, Governor of the Seltnafugal islands

Chapter 15
- *Das Mittagessen ist fast fertig!* Lunch is nearly ready!
- *Habt ihr Brot mitgebracht?* Did you bring any bread back with you?
- *O Entschuldigung, das haben wir vergessen.* Oh sorry, we forgot.
- *Das macht nichts.* It doesn't matter.
- *Wir müssen auf Vati warten. Er kommt gleich.* We have to wait for Dad. He's just coming.
- *Hast du das Tagebuch?* Have you got the diary?
- *Nein, ich habe es in mein Zelt gelegt. Bleibt hier!* No, I put it in my tent. Wait here!
- *Ach... Hier erklärt er, wie er Tobias Blumenkohls Brief gefunden hat.* Oh... Here he explains how he found Tobias Blumenkohl's letter.
- *Er suchte blaue Papageien...* He was looking for blue parrots...
- *Er hat es geschafft, die Kuckuck-Insel zu erreichen.* He managed to get to Kuckuck island.
- *Am Eingang zu einer Höhle hat er eine rostige, alte Kiste gesehen.* At the entrance to a cave he saw a rusty old chest.
- *Darin hat er einen Brief gefunden, der von einem Schatz sprach.* Inside, he found a letter that talked about treasure.
- *Ja, das war der Brief, den er gestohlen hat.* Yes, that was the letter he stole.
- *Zu Tisch! Hier kommt Vati.* Come and sit down! Here comes Dad.
- *Entschuldigung, ich habe eine sehr lange Sitzung gehabt.* Sorry, I had a very long meeting.

Chapter 16
- *Wir müssen zum Dreieich-Bauernhof gehen...* We have to go to Dreieich farm...
- *...um den Mann mit der Glatze und den Hinweis aus der Schule zu suchen.* ...to look for the bald man and the clue from the school.
- *Kaffee, Herr Speck?* Coffee, Mr Speck?
- *Danke schön... Äh, ich wollte Sie etwas fragen.* Thank you... Er, I wanted to ask you something.
- *Heute Morgen bin ich nach Turmstadt gefahren. Ich habe das Schloss und die zwei Türme gesehen...* I went to Turmstadt this morning. I saw the castle and the two towers...

Chapters 16 to 19

- *...aber den zerstörten Turm habe ich nicht gefunden.* ...but I didn't find the ruined tower.
- *Warum wollen Sie den sehen? Es sind nur alte Steine.* Why do you want to see that? It's only old stones.
- *Äh...ich mag Ruinen.* Er...I like ruins.
- *Na, sind Sie in den Park gegangen?* Well, did you go to the park?
- *Ja, aber ich habe dort nichts gesehen.* Yes, but I didn't see anything there.
- *Aha, Sie sind nicht bis zum Fluss hinuntergegangen.* Ah, you didn't go right down to the river.
- *Hallo Elke, wie geht's?* Hi Elke, how are you?
- *...Ja, der alte Turm ist am Fluss.* ...Yes, the old tower is by the river.
- *Ach, wirklich? Das ist sehr interessant.* Oh really... That's very interesting.
- *Der nächste Hinweis muss im alten Turm sein.* The next clue must be in the old tower.

Chapter 17

- *Er hat also den Hinweis aus der Schule entziffert...* So, he's worked out the clue from the school...
- *...und der hat ihn zum alten Turm geschickt.* ...and that sent him to the old tower.
- *Aber er hat ihn noch nicht gefunden.* But he hasn't found it yet.
- *Wir müssen also sofort dahin - vor ihm.* So we must go there straight away - before him.
- *Nehmen wir unsere Fahrräder!* Let's take our bikes!
- *Wegen des Zaunes habe ich den Turm nie richtig erforscht.* I've never really explored the tower properly because of the fence.
- *Nichts! Ich hab' überall gesucht und jeden Stein untersucht.* Nothing! I've looked everywhere and examined every stone.
- *Mensch! Ich hab' hier etwas gefunden.* Hey! I've found something here!
- *Schaut! Das ist Tobias Blumenkohls Zeichen!* Look! It's Tobias Blumenkohl's sign!

The writing on the tower:
We have kept this old tower as a monument for the inhabitants of Turmstadt. The pirates of Pirates' island destroyed it three years ago, but now we have got our revenge. We have won our last battle against them. We have driven them out of their fort on the island and they have disappeared from our country.

Chapter 18

- *Also, wir müssen zur Pirateninsel fahren.* So we must go to Pirates' island.
- *Wir werden doch zu spät ankommen. Heute geht's nicht.* But we'll get there too late. Today's no good.
- *Aber hier wird der Mann den Hinweis finden und...er wird vielleicht während der Nacht zur Insel fahren.* But the man will find the clue here and...he might go to the island during the night.
- *Also, dann müssen wir diesen Hinweis mit Laub verdecken. So!* Well then, we must hide this clue with leaves. There!
- *Wir können auch eine falsche Spur hinterlassen.* We can also leave a false trail.
- *Großartig! Er wird in die falsche Richtung gehen und uns nicht stören.* Brilliant!

He'll go in the wrong direction and won't disturb us.
- *Na gut, wir müssen ihm einen Zettel dalassen.* Right, we must leave him a note here.
- *Ich habe eine gute Idee.* I've got a good idea.
- *Aber wo werden wir ihn verstecken?* But where shall we hide it?
- *Erich und ich können ein gutes Versteck suchen.* Erich and I can look for a good hiding-place.
- *Wir können ihn hier verstecken und sein Zeichen darauf setzen.* We can hide it here and put his sign on there.
- *Das ist wirklich großartig! Darauf wird er bestimmt hereinfallen.* That's really brilliant! He'll definitely fall for it.

The false trail:

Mein lieber Sohn, nun hast du alle Hinweise gefunden, die ich hinterlassen habe. Hier ist deine letzte Aufgabe. Sie wird schwierig sein. Du wirst zur Polizeiwache in Alterhaven gehen müssen. Dort wirst du ein Fenster ohne Gitter sehen. Auf diese Weise wirst du hineingehen. Drinnen wirst du eine mit Holzplatten verkleidete Wand sehen. Dort wirst du alle meine Juwelen und mein Vermögen finden. Leb wohl, T.B.

My dear son, Now you have found all the clues I left behind. Here is your last task. It will be difficult. You will have to go to the police station in Alterhaven. You will see one window without bars. You will go in that way. Inside you will see a wall with wooden panels. There you will find all my jewels and my fortune. Farewell, T.B.

Chapter 19

- *Wir machen jetzt zu.* We're going to close up now.
- *In Ordnung. Ich gehe auch bald nach Hause.* Fine. I'm going home soon as well.
- *He! Das ist der Mann, den mir die Kinder gezeigt haben.* Hey! That's the man the children showed me.
- *Ja, das ist derselbe Mann.* Yes, that's the same man.
- *Hallo, Berlin? Ich möchte weitere Einzelheiten über Nummer 7454.* Hello, Berlin? I'd like further details about number 7454.
- *Gut, ich seh' mal nach und dann werde ich alles an Sie durchfaxen.* Right, I'll have a look and then I'll fax everything through to you.
- *Sehr gut. Auf Wiederhören.* Great. Goodbye.
- *Ah, es ist dieses hier. Die da haben alle Gitter.* Ah, it's this one here. Those all have bars.
- *Gut, das wird nicht schwierig sein. Ich werde die Fensterscheibe einschlagen können.* Right, that won't be difficult. I'll be able to break the window pane.
- *Ich gehe zuerst essen und, wenn es wirklich dunkel ist, komme ich zurück.* First I'll go and eat, and I'll come back when it's really dark.
- *Ah, endlich...* Ah, at last...
- *Also, morgen gehe ich zum Blumenkohl-Haus.* Right, tomorrow I'll go to the Blumenkohl house.
- *Die Kinder werden mir vielleicht helfen können, ihn zu finden.* Perhaps the children will be able to help me find him.
- *Oh! Was war denn das?* Oh! What was that?
- *Er ist's! Äh... Halt! Sie sind verhaftet.* It's him! Er...Stop! You're under arrest.

Chapters 20 to 22

Chapter 20

- *Kannst du mir dein Handtuch leihen?* Can you lend me your towel?
- *Pfui! Es ist genauso nass wie meins.* Yuk! It's just as wet as mine.
- *Hallo, Ralf! Hast du dein Boot hier?* Hallo Ralf! Have you got your boat here?
- *Ja, es ist da drüben.* Yes, it's over there.
- *Können wir es uns leihen? Wir wollen auf die Pirateninsel.* Can we borrow it? We want to go to Pirates' island.
- *Ja, natürlich. Es ist das kleinste.* Yes, of course. It's the smallest one.
- *Passt auf! Ein Ruder ist kürzer als das andere...* Watch out, one of the oars is shorter than the other...
- *He! Wir beginnen uns im Kreis zu drehen.* Hey! We're starting to go around in circles.
- *Ja, Erich! Du ruderst nicht so schnell wie ich.* Yes, Erich! You're not rowing as fast as me.
- *Du hast das bessere Ruder.* You've got the best oar.
- *Nein, hab' ich nicht. Ich bin einfach kräftiger als du.* No I haven't, I'm just stronger than you!
- *Da ist die Festung.* There's the fort.
- *Sie ist noch älter als der alte Turm.* It's even older than the old tower.
- *Sie hat viele Kerker und Tunnel...* It's got lots of dungeons and tunnels...
- *...aber man kann da nicht hinunter.* ...but you can't go down there.
- *Komisch. Das Tor ist normalerweise zu.* That's odd. The gate's normally shut.
- *Ich gehe lieber nicht hinunter.* I'd rather not go down.
- *Ach, Mensch!* Oh no!
- *Schaut mal, es gibt vier Tunnel.* Look, there are four tunnels.
- *Oh, nein!* Oh no!
- *Wir können nicht mehr hinaus!* We can't get out any more!
- *Kommt hierher! Schaut euch das mal an!* Come here! Take a look at this!
- *Mein Tunnel ist nicht so lang wie deiner.* My tunnel isn't as long as yours.
- *Mein erster Tunnel war genauso lang wie deiner, aber mein zweiter Tunnel ist kürzer.* My first tunnel was just as long as yours, but my second one is shorter.
- *Meiner ist länger als Tanjas erster Tunnel.* Mine is longer than Tanja's first tunnel.

Chapter 21

- *Wenn der Schatz hier ist, finden wir ihn!* If the treasure's here, we'll find it!
- *Nichts! Der Tunnel endet hier.* Nothing! The tunnel ends here.
- *Wäre es besser, wenn du die Taschenlampe hättest?* Would it be better if you had the torch?
- *Ja. Reich sie mir!* Yes, pass it to me!
- *Oh! Es gibt hier einen eisernen Ring an der Mauer. Ich ziehe daran.* Oh, there's an iron ring in the wall here. I'm going to give it a pull.
- *Mensch!* Wow!
- *Guten Tag, ich möchte mit Monika, Erich und Tanja sprechen.* Hello, I'd like to talk to Monika, Erich and Tanja.
- *Ich möchte ihnen danken. Sie haben mir geholfen, einen Verbrecher zu schnappen!* I'd like to thank them. They helped me catch a criminal!

- *Möchten Sie auf sie warten?* Would you like to wait for them?
- *Nein, ich werde zurückkommen. Ich möchte Sie nicht stören.* No, I'll come back. I wouldn't like to disturb you.
- *Aber zuerst könnten Sie uns vielleicht die ganze Geschichte erzählen. Wir wissen nichts!* But first, perhaps you could tell us the whole story. We don't know anything!

Chapter 22
- *Also... Wir sollten einen Ausgang suchen.* Right... We should look for a way out.
- *Vielleicht finden wir einen, wenn wir zur Treppe zurückgehen.* We might find one if we go back to the steps.
- *Schaut mal! Licht!* Look! Light!
- *Puh!* Phew!
- *Tanja, wenn du die großen Steine da vorschiebst, sieht niemand die Spalte.* Tanja, if you push those rocks in front, nobody'll see the crack.
- *Jetzt kann ich Ralf neue Ruder kaufen.* Now I can buy Ralph some new oars.

Monika's letter:
Monday, September 2
Dear Tanja and Erich, Here's the article from the Courier that tells our story. It's brilliant! What are you doing with your share of the reward? I'm going to buy a CD player with mine. If your mother agrees, I'll visit you during the Christmas holidays. So see you soon I hope! Love from Monika

The newspaper article:
Friday, August 30

The Blumenkohl family treasure.

Monika Blumenkohl with her friends Erich and Tanja Müller and her dog, Hüpfer. Stefan Speck, the rare-bird thief who wanted to steal the Blumenkohl treasure.

The month of August has been an exciting time for Monika Blumenkohl and her friends Erich and Tanja. They found some treasure and helped the police catch the criminal Stefan Speck.
Many years ago, Monika's great-grandfather, Tobias, died on a remote island. He left behind a chest. This chest was hidden beside the entrance to a cave. A few months ago, Speck was on the same island. He was looking for some very rare parrots there that he wanted to steal.
By chance, he came across the old chest and found a letter from Tobias in it. The letter was addressed to Georg, Monika's grandfather. It was the first clue in a treasure hunt and brought Speck to Turmstadt, where he stupidly lost it. Erich and Tanja, who were just arriving to spend a few days with their friend Monika, found it. The three young people managed to find the treasure (gold), hidden in the old pirates' fort, before the criminal could do so. They also helped the police catch Speck. The three heroes also received a reward of 2,000 euros from the police. Our congratulations to them!

Irregular and modal verbs

This table lists the most common irregular German verbs and the six modal verbs. The first column shows the infinitive of the verb, followed by the three different imperatives (*du, ihr* and *Sie* forms), and then the past participle (p.p.). If a verb uses *sein* to make the perfect tense, then it will say "with *sein*" after the past participle. The subjunctive is the "would" form of the verb, for example "I would like". To make the future tense, you use the present tense of *werden* and the infinitive of the verb.

	Present tense	Imperfect tense	Subjunctive
haben (to have)	ich habe	ich hatte	ich hätte
	du hast	du hattest	du hättest
hab! habt! haben Sie!	er/sie/es hat	es/sie/es hatte	er/sie/es hätte
	wir haben	wir hatten	wir hätten
past participle: *gehabt*	ihr habt	ihr hattet	ihr hättet
	sie haben	sie hatten	sie hätten
	Sie haben	Sie hatten	Sie hätten
sein (to be)	ich bin	ich war	ich wäre
	du bist	du warst	du wärst
sei! seid! seien Sie!	er/sie/es ist	er/sie/es war	er/sie/es wäre
	wir sind	wir waren	wir wären
p.p. *gewesen*	ihr seid	ihr wart	ihr wäret
(with *sein*)	sie sind	sie waren	sie wären
	Sie sind	Sie waren	Sie wären
tun (to do)	ich tu(e)	ich tat	ich täte
	du tust	du tatest	du tätest
tu(e)! tut! tun Sie!	er/sie/es tut	er/sie/es tat	er/sie/es täte
	wir tun	wir taten	wir täten
p.p. *getan*	ihr tut	ihr tatet	ihr tätet
	sie tun	sie taten	sie täten
	Sie tun	Sie taten	Sie täten
werden (to become)	ich werde	ich wurde	ich würde
	du wirst	du wurdest	du würdest
werde! werdet! werden Sie!	er/sie/es wird	er/sie/es wurde	er/sie/es würde
	wir werden	wir wurden	wir würden
p.p. *geworden*	ihr werdet	ihr wurdet	ihr würdet
(with *sein*)	sie werden	sie wurden	sie würden
	Sie werden	Sie wurden	Sie würden
wissen (to know)	ich weiß	ich wusste	ich wüsste
	du weißt	du wusstest	du wüsstest
wisse! wisset! wissen Sie!	er/sie/es weiß	er/sie/es wusste	er/sie/es wüsste
	wir wissen	wir wussten	wir wüssten
	ihr wisst	ihr wusstet	ihr wüsstet
p.p. *gewusst*	sie wissen	sie wussten	sie wüssten
	Sie wissen	Sie wussten	Sie wüssten

The six modal verbs

	Present tense	Imperfect tense	Subjunctive
dürfen (may, to be allowed to)	*ich darf*	*ich durfte*	*ich dürfte*
	du darfst	*du durftest*	*du dürftest*
	er/sie/es darf	*er/sie/es durfte*	*er/sie/es dürfte*
p.p. *gedurft*	*wir dürfen*	*wir durften*	*wir dürften*
	ihr dürft	*ihr durftet*	*ihr dürftet*
	sie dürfen	*sie durften*	*sie dürften*
	Sie dürfen	*Sie durften*	*Sie dürften*
können (can, to be able to)	*ich kann*	*ich konnte*	*ich könnte*
	du kannst	*du konntest*	*du könntest*
	er/sie/es kann	*er/sie/es konnte*	*er/sie/es könnte*
p.p. *gekonnt*	*wir können*	*wir konnten*	*wir könnten*
	ihr könnt	*ihr konntet*	*ihr könntet*
	sie können	*sie konnten*	*sie könnten*
	Sie können	*Sie konnten*	*Sie könnten*
mögen (to like)	*ich mag*	*ich mochte*	*ich möchte*
	du magst	*du mochtest*	*du möchtest*
p.p. *gemocht*	*er/sie/es mag*	*er/sie/es mochte*	*er/sie/es möchte*
	wir mögen	*wir mochten*	*wir möchten*
	ihr mögt	*ihr mochtet*	*ihr möchtet*
	sie mögen	*sie mochten*	*sie möchten*
	Sie mögen	*Sie mochten*	*Sie möchten*
müssen (must, to have to)	*ich muss*	*ich musste*	*ich müsste*
	du musst	*du musstest*	*du müsstest*
	er/sie/es muss	*er/sie/es musste*	*er/sie/es müsste*
p.p. *gemusst*	*wir müssen*	*wir mussten*	*wir müssten*
	ihr müsst	*ihr musstet*	*ihr müsstet*
	sie müssen	*sie mussten*	*sie müssten*
	Sie müssen	*Sie mussten*	*Sie müssten*
sollen (should, to be supposed to)	*ich soll*	*ich sollte*	*ich sollte*
	du sollst	*du solltest*	*du solltest*
	er/sie/es soll	*er/sie/es sollte*	*er/sie/es sollte*
p.p. *gesollt*	*wir sollen*	*wir sollten*	*wir sollten*
	ihr sollt	*ihr solltet*	*ihr solltet*
	sie sollen	*sie sollten*	*sie sollten*
	Sie sollen	*Sie sollten*	*Sie sollten*
wollen (to want)	*ich will*	*ich wollte*	*ich wollte*
	du willst	*du wolltest*	*du wolltest*
p.p. *gewollt*	*er/sie/es will*	*er/sie/es wollte*	*er/sie/es wollte*
	wir wollen	*wir wollten*	*wir wollten*
	ihr wollt	*ihr wolltet*	*ihr wolltet*
	sie wollen	*sie wollten*	*sie wollten*
	Sie wollen	*Sie wollten*	*Sie wollten*

Strong and mixed verbs

These tables list most of the strong and mixed verbs that are commonly used in German. The present tense *er* form tells you if the verb has a vowel change with *du* and *er/sie/es*. The imperfect tense *er* form gives you the stem for the imperfect. Verbs which use *sein* in the perfect tense are listed separately.

Strong verbs with *haben*

Infinitive	Present	Imperfect	Perfect	
beginnen	beginnt	begann	hat begonnen	to begin, to start
bekommen	bekommt	bekam	hat bekommen	to receive, to get
bitten	bittet	bat	hat gebeten	to request, to ask
brechen	bricht	brach	hat gebrochen	to break
empfehlen	empfiehlt	empfahl	hat empfohlen	to recommend
essen	isst	aß	hat gegessen	to eat
fangen	fängt	fing	hat gefangen	to catch
finden	findet	fand	hat gefunden	to find
geben	gibt	gab	hat gegeben	to give
genießen	genießt	genoss	hat genossen	to enjoy
gewinnen	gewinnt	gewann	hat gewonnen	to win
halten	hält	hielt	hat gehalten	to stop, to hold
heißen	heißt	hieß	hat geheißen	to be called
helfen	hilft	half	hat geholfen	to help
lassen	lässt	ließ	hat gelassen	to let, to leave
leihen	leiht	lieh	hat geliehen	to lend
lesen	liest	las	hat gelesen	to read
nehmen	nimmt	nahm	hat genommen	to take
rufen	ruft	rief	hat gerufen	to call
schieben	schiebt	schob	hat geschoben	to push, to shove
schlafen	schläft	schlief	hat geschlafen	to sleep
schlagen	schlägt	schlug	hat geschlagen	to hit, to strike
schließen	schließt	schloss	hat geschlossen	to shut
schneiden	schneidet	schnitt	hat geschnitten	to cut
schreiben	schreibt	schrieb	hat geschrieben	to write
schreien	schreit	schrie	hat geschrien	to shout
sehen	sieht	sah	hat gesehen	to see
singen	singt	sang	hat gesungen	to sing
sitzen	sitzt	saß	hat gesessen	to sit
sprechen	spricht	sprach	hat gesprochen	to speak
stehen	steht	stand	hat gestanden	to stand
stehlen	stiehlt	stahl	hat gestohlen	to steal
tragen	trägt	trug	hat getragen	to carry
treffen	trifft	traf	hat getroffen	to meet
trinken	trinkt	trank	hat getrunken	to drink
vergessen	vergisst	vergaß	hat vergessen	to forget
verlieren	verliert	verlor	hat verloren	to lose
waschen	wäscht	wusch	hat gewaschen	to wash
werfen	wirft	warf	hat geworfen	to throw
ziehen	zieht	zog	hat gezogen	to pull

Strong verbs with *sein*

Infinitive	Present	Imperfect	Perfect	
bleiben	bleibt	blieb	ist geblieben	to stay
fahren	fährt	fuhr	ist gefahren	to go, to drive
fallen	fällt	fiel	ist gefallen	to fall
fliegen	fliegt	flog	ist geflogen	to fly
gehen	geht	ging	ist gegangen	to go, to walk
geschehen	geschieht	geschah	ist geschehen	to happen
kommen	kommt	kam	ist gekommen	to come
laufen	läuft	lief	ist gelaufen	to run
schwimmen	schwimmt	schwamm	ist geschwommen	to swim
springen	springt	sprang	ist gesprungen	to jump
steigen	steigt	stieg	ist gestiegen	to climb
sterben	stirbt	starb	ist gestorben	to die
wachsen	wächst	wuchs	ist gewachsen	to grow

Mixed verbs

Mixed verbs are a mixture of strong and weak verbs. Like strong verbs, they have an irregular imperfect stem, but they add weak verb endings.

Infinitive	Present	Imperfect	Perfect	
brennen	brennt	brannte	hat gebrannt	to burn
bringen	bringt	brachte	hat gebracht	to bring
denken	denkt	dachte	hat gedacht	to think
kennen	kennt	kannte	hat gekannt	to know
senden	sendet	sandte	hat gesandt	to send

Word order with verbs

In a simple German clause, the verb must be the second element in the clause. This often means you have to turn the subject and verb around:

e.g. *Im Winter **fahre ich** gern Ski.*
(In the winter, I like to go skiing.)

You do **not** need to turn the subject and verb around if they follow any of these words:

und (and), *aber* (but), *oder* (or), *sondern* (but), *denn* (for)

e.g. *Ich habe Sport gern **und ich spiele** oft Tennis.*
(I like sport and I often play tennis.)

Verb to the end

After the following words, the verb must go to the end of the clause:

als	when (past events)
bevor	before
bis	until
da	since (because)
dass	that
nachdem	after
ob	whether
obwohl	although
seit	since (time)
während	while
weil	because
wenn	if, when(ever)

e.g. *...weil ich in die Stadt **fahre**.*
(...because I'm going into town.)

Vocabulary list: a - e

Here is a list of the German words used in this book, along with their English translations.

Nouns

The plural endings of nouns are shown in brackets. Add the letter(s) in brackets to the noun to get the plural form, e.g. the plural of **der Brief(-e)** is **die Briefe**.

Abbreviations

acc means accusative
gen means genitive
dat means dative
pl means plural

Verbs

An asterisk (*) after a verb indicates that it is a strong verb. You can find a list of strong verbs and their vowel changes on pages 114-115.

A cross (†) indicates that a verb is irregular. Irregular verbs are written out in full on pages 112-113.

Separable verbs are shown like this: **auf'passen**. See page 36 for more about separable verbs.

A

abends	in the evening(s)
aber	but
ab'geben*	to hand in
abgeschlossen	locked
ab'hauen	to clear off
ab'holen	to fetch
die Adresse(-n)	address
Afrika	Africa
die Aktentasche(-n)	briefcase
alle	all
allein	alone
allerseits	(to) everyone
alles	everything
als	as (a), than, when
also	well then, right, so
alt	old
am	(short for **an dem**)
Amerika	America
die Ampel(-n)	set of traffic lights
sich amüsieren	to enjoy yourself, to have fun
an [+ acc or dat]	on, at
an'beten	to worship
der/die/das andere	the other
an'fangen*	to start, to begin
an'kommen*	to arrive
ans	(short for **an das**)
an'schauen	to (go and) look at
sich (etwas) an'schauen	to (take a) look at (something)
an'sehen*	to look at
der Anteil(-e)	share, portion
die Antwort(-en)	answer
sich an'ziehen*	to get dressed
der Anzug(-¨e)	suit

der Apfel(-¨)	apple
die Apotheke(-n)	pharmacy
arbeiten	to work
sich ärgern	to be/get annoyed
der Artikel(-)	article
das Atelier(-s)	studio
auch	too, also
auf [+ acc or dat]	on, onto, on top of, in (a language), up
auf diese Weise	(in) this way
auf'essen*	to eat up, to finish
die Aufgabe(-n)	task
auf'passen	to watch out, to pay attention
auf'räumen	to tidy up
aufs	(short for **auf das**)
auf'stehen*	to get up
auf'wachen	to wake up
aus [+ dat]	out of, from
der Ausflug(-¨e)	outing, trip
der Ausgang(-¨e)	exit
aus'geben*	to spend (money)
sich aus'ruhen	to have a rest, to relax
aus'sehen*	to seem, to look

B

die Bäckerei(-en)	bakery
der Bahnhof(-¨e)	station
bald	soon
das Band(-¨er)	ribbon
die Bank(-¨e)	bench
bauen	to build
der Bauernhof(-¨e)	farm
der Baum(-¨e)	tree

sich beeilen	to hurry	da drüben	there, over there
sich befinden*	to be, to be situated	das Dach(-̈er)	roof
begegnen [+ dat]	to meet (bump into)	dahin	(to) there
beginnen*	to begin, to start	da'lassen*	to leave here/there
bei [+ dat]	near, at ...'s house	danke	thank you, thanks
beim	(short for **bei dem**)	danke schön	thank you
die beiden	both	dann	then
bekommen*	to receive, to get, to have (babies)	das geht	it's all right
		das ist	that is, it's
bellen	to bark	das macht nichts	it doesn't matter
die Belohnung(-en)	reward	das stimmt	that's right/true
benutzen	to use	dein/deine	your
der Berg(-e)	mountain	denken	to think
sich beruhigen	to calm down	das Denkmal(-̈er)	monument
beschädigen	to damage	denn	for, because, then
besorgen	to get, to acquire	der/die/das/die	the
besser	better	derselbe/dieselbe/	the (very) same
der/die/das beste	the best	dasselbe/dieselben	
bestimmt	definitely	dich	you, yourself
das Bett(-en)	bed	der Dieb(-e)	thief
bevor	before	diese	these
das Bild(-er)	picture	diese da	those
bis [+ acc]	until, as far as	dieser/diese/dieses	this, that, this/that one
bis bald	see you soon	doch	yet, but
bis später	see you later	der Dom(-e)	cathedral
bitte	please	doof	stupid, silly
bitten* um [+ acc]	to ask for	das Dorf(-̈er)	village
blau	blue	dort	there
bleiben*	to stay, to keep	dort drüben	there, over there
bloß	merely, only	draußen	outside
der Blumenkohl(-e)	cauliflower	dreckig	filthy, horrible
das Bonbon(-s)	sweet, candy	sich drehen	to turn, to go around
das Boot(-e)	boat	drinnen	inside
der Botaniker(-)	botanist	dritt- [+ ending]	third
braun	brown	du	you
brav	good, well behaved	dumm	stupid
der Brief(-e)	letter	dummerweise	stupidly
die Brille(-n)	(pair of) glasses	dunkel	dark
bringen	to bring, to take	durch [+ acc]	through
das Brot(-e)	bread, loaf	durch'faxen	to fax through
das Brötchen(-)	(bread) roll	dürfen†	to be allowed to, may
die Brücke(-n)	bridge		
der Bruder(-̈)	brother	**E**	
der Brunnen(-)	fountain		
das Buch(-̈er)	book	eben	just
der Buntstift(-e)	coloured pencil	echt	genuine, real
		eher	sooner
C		die Ehre(-n)	honour
		die Eiche(-n)	oak (tree)
das Café(-s)	café	ein/eine	a
der Campingplatz(-̈e)	campsite	ein bisschen	a bit/little
die Cola(-s)	cola	der Einbrecher(-)	burglar
		einfach	simply, just
D		der Eingang(-̈e)	entrance
		einige	some, a few
da	there	ein'kaufen	to do some shopping

Vocabulary list: e - j

einkaufen gehen*	to go shopping
ein'schlagen*	to break, to smash in
ein'stellen	to put away/in
einverstanden sein	to agree
der Einwohner(-)	inhabitant
die Einzelheit(-en)	detail
das Eis	ice-cream
eisern	iron
eiskalt	ice-cold
die Eltern [pl]	parents
empfehlen*	to recommend
das Ende	end
enden	to end
endlich	at last
[acc +] entlang	along, alongside
entlegen	remote, isolated
entschuldige, entschuldigen Sie	excuse me
Entschuldigung	excuse me, sorry
entziffern	to decipher, to figure out
er	he/it
die Erdbeere(-n)	strawberry
die Erde	earth, soil, world
erforschen	to explore
erhalten*	to preserve, to keep
erklären	to explain
erreichen	to reach
erscheinen*	to appear, to seem
erst	not until, only
der/die/das erste	the first
erzählen	to tell, to talk
es geht ihnen gut	they're fine
es geht nicht	it's no good, it won't work
es gibt	there is/are
es ist	it is, there is
essen*	to eat
etwas	something
euer/eure	your
der Euro(-)	euro

F

fahren*	to go, to drive, to travel
das Fahrrad(-̈er)	bicycle
der Fahrschein(-e)	ticket
fallen*	to fall
fallen lassen*	to drop
falsch	false, wrong
die Familie(-n)	family
fangen*	to catch
fassen	to catch, to apprehend
fehlen	to be missing
das Fenster(-)	window

die Fensterscheibe(-n)	window-pane
die Ferien [pl]	holidays
das Fernglas(-̈er)	(pair of) binoculars
fertig	ready, finished
fest	tight, hard
die Festung(-en)	fort, fortress
der Film(-e)	film
finden*	to find
fliegen*	to fly
der Flughafen(-̈)	airport
der Fluss(-̈e)	river
folgen [+ dat]	to follow
das Foto(-s)	photo
der Fotoapparat(-e)	camera
das Fotokopier-gerät(-e)	photocopier
Fotos machen	to take photos
die Frage(-n)	question
fragen	to ask
die Frau(-en)	woman
Fräulein	Miss
frei	free
der Freund(-e)	friend (boy)
die Freundin(-nen)	friend (girl)
das Frühstück(-e)	breakfast
sich (wohl) fühlen	to feel (well, happy)
für [+ acc]	for
der Fußball(-̈e)	football
der Fußgänger(-)	pedestrian
der Fußgänger-überweg(-e)	pedestrian crossing

G

ganz	entire(ly), whole, quite
ganz allein	all alone
gar nicht	not at all
der Garten(-̈)	garden
der Gauner(-)	crook, scoundrel
das Gebäude(-)	building
geben*	to give
gefährlich	dangerous
gegen [+ acc]	against, towards
die Gegend(-en)	area, region
gegenüber [+ dat]	opposite
das Geheimnis(-se)	secret
gehen*	to go, to walk
gehören [+dat]	to belong to
gelb	yellow
das Geld	money
gelingen*	to succeed
das Gemüse	vegetables
gemütlich	cosy, friendly, pleasant
genau	exactly, exact
(genau)so...wie	(just) as...as
genießen*	to enjoy

das Gepäck	luggage
gerade	just
geradeaus	straight ahead
gern	gladly
das Geschäft(-e)	shop
geschehen*	to happen
die Geschichte(-n)	story, history
geschlossen	closed
das Gesicht(-er)	face
gestern	yesterday
gestern Abend	yesterday evening, last night
gestohlen	stolen
das Gitter(-)	grid, bars
die Glatze(-n)	bald head, bald patch
gleich	right away, (the) same
Glück haben	to be lucky
das Gold	gold
der Gouverneur(-e)	governor
gratulieren [+dat]	to congratulate (someone)
grau	grey
groß	big, tall
großartig	brilliant, wonderful
die Großmutter(-ˉ)	grandmother
der Großvater(-ˉ)	grandfather
grün	green
gut	good, well
guten Abend	good evening
guten Tag	hello

H

haben†	to have
der Hafen(-ˉ)	port, harbour
halb eins	half past twelve
halb zwei	half past one
hallo	hello, hi
halt!	stop!
die Hand(-ˉe)	hand
das Handtuch(-ˉer)	towel
der Handwerker(-)	workman
das Haus(-ˉer)	house
heißen*	to be called
der Held(-en)	hero
helfen* [+ dat]	to help
das Hemd(-en)	shirt
herein'fallen* auf [+ acc]	to fall for (something)
herein'tragen*	to carry in
Herrn	to Mr
herrschen	to be (for weather)
herüber	over here
heute	today
heute Abend	this evening, tonight
heute Morgen	this morning

hier	here
hier spricht	it's (here speaks)
hierher	(towards) here
der Himmel	sky
hin und wieder	now and again
hinein'gehen*	to go in, to come in
hinein'kommen*	to come in, to get in
hinter [+ acc or dat]	behind
hinterlassen*	to leave behind
hinunter'gehen*	to go down
der Hinweis(-e)	clue, tip
(höchst-) wahrscheinlich	(most) probably
hoffentlich	hopefully
die Höhle(-n)	cave
holen	to fetch
die Hose(-n)	(pair of) trousers
die Hosen-tasche(-n)	trouser pocket
das Hotel(-s)	hotel
hübsch	pretty
der Hügel(-)	hill
der Hund(-e)	dog
der Hüpfer(-)	hop, skip

I

ich	I
ideal	perfect, ideal
die Idee(-n)	idea
im	(short for in dem)
im Kreis	in a circle, in circles
im Schatten	in the shade
immer	always
in [+ acc or dat]	in, into
in der Nähe von [+ dat]	near
in Ordnung	fine, OK
der Inhaber(-)	proprietor, owner
ins	(short for in das)
die Insel(-n)	island
die Inselgruppe(-n)	group of islands
interessant	interesting
irgendwo	somewhere

J

ja	yes
die Jacke(-n)	jacket
das Jahr(-e)	year
...Jahre alt	...years old
die Jeans [pl]	jeans
jedenfalls	anyhow
jetzt	now
jung	young
das Juwel(-en)	jewel

Vocabulary list: k - s

K

der Kaffee(-s)	coffee
der Kai(-e or -s)	quay
der Kampf(-¨e)	battle, struggle
kaputt	broken
die Karte(-n)	map, card, ticket
der Karton(-s)	cardboard box
der Käse(-)	cheese
die Katze(-n)	cat
kaufen	to buy
kein/keine	not a, not any, no
keine Sorge!	don't worry!
kennen	to know
der Kerker(-)	dungeon
die Kerze(-n)	candle
das Kilo	kilo
das Kind(-er)	child, kid
das Kino(-s)	cinema
die Kirche(-n)	church
die Kiste(-n)	chest, case, crate
klar	clear
klasse!	great!
das Kleid(-er)	dress
die Kleider [pl]	clothes
klein	small, short
klettern	to climb, to clamber
der Koffer(-)	suitcase
der Kollege(-n)	colleague
komisch	funny, strange, odd
kommen*	to come
können†	to be able to, can
die Kopfschmerz-tablette(-n)	aspirin, headache pill
der Korb(-¨e)	basket
kosten	to cost
kräftig	strong, powerful
krank	ill
der Kratzer(-)	scratch
der Krebs(-e)	crab
die Kreuzung(-en)	crossroads, junction
der Kuchen(-)	cake
die Kuh(-¨e)	cow
der Kumpel(-)	mate, good friend
der Kurier(-e)	courier
kurz	short
die Küste(-n)	coast

L

lachen	to laugh
das Land(-¨er)	country, land
die Landkarte(-n)	map
die Landschaft [no pl]	countryside, scenery
lang	long
langsam	slow(ly)

das Laub [no pl]	leaves, foliage
laufen*	to run, to walk
laut	loud(ly)
leb wohl	farewell
leer	empty
legen	to put (lay down)
der Lehrer(-)	teacher
leicht	easy, light
leichter Diebstahl [m]	petty theft
leider	unfortunately
leihen*	to rent, to lend
sich (etwas) leihen*	to borrow (something)
lesen*	to read
der/die/das letzte	the last
die Leute [pl]	people
das Licht(-er)	light
lieb	dear
Lieber [+ m name], Liebe [+ f name]	Dear...
lieber	more gladly, preferabl
Liebling	darling, dear
Lieblings-	favourite (adds on to front of noun)
die Limonade(-n)	lemonade
links	(on the) left
der Lohn(-¨e)	wage, fee
die Luft	air
die Lupe(-n)	magnifying glass

M

machen	to do, to make
man	one, you
der Mann(-¨er)	man
der Markt(-¨e)	market
die Mauer(-n)	wall (outside)
der Mechaniker(-)	mechanic
das Meer(-e)	sea
mehr	more
der/die/das meiste	(the) most
Mensch!	Hey! Wow! Man!
mich	myself, me
mit [+ dat]	with
mit Holzplatten verkleidet	with wooden panels
mit'bringen	to bring along/with
mit'kommen*	to come along/with
Mittag	midday, noon
das Mittagessen(-)	lunch
Mitternacht	midnight
mögen†	to like
der Monat(-e)	month
morgen	tomorrow
morgen früh	tomorrow morning
morgens	in the morning(s)
müde	tired

die Mühe(-n)	trouble, effort
müssen†	to have to, must
die Mutter(-¨)	mother
Mutti	Mum(my)
die Mütze(-n)	cap

N

na	now then, well
na gut	right, well, OK
nach [+ dat]	after, to (used with a place name)
nach Hause	(to) home
nach links/rechts	(to the) left/right
der Nachbar(-n)	neighbour
nach'denken	to think, to ponder
nachmittags	in the afternoon(s)
nach'sehen*	to have a look
der/die/das nächste	the nearest/next
die Nacht(-¨e)	night
die Nagelfeile(-n)	nail file
nah	near
die Nähe [no pl]	vicinity
näher	nearer
namens	called
nass	wet
natürlich	of course, naturally
neben [+acc or dat]	next to, beside
nehmen*	to take
nein	no
nett	nice, kind
das Netz(-e)	net
neu	new
nicht	not
nicht mehr	not any more, no longer
nichts	nothing
nie(mals)	never
niemand	nobody, no one
noch	still
noch nicht	not yet
nomalerweise	normally
die Nummer(-n)	number
nun	now
nur	only

O

ohne [+ acc]	without
das Ohr(-en)	ear
oje!	oh dear! oh no!
die Orange(-n)	orange
der Orangensaft(-¨e)	orange juice

P

das Paar(-e)	pair, couple
der Papagei(-en)	parrot
das Papier(-e)	paper
der Park(-s)	park
passieren	to happen
(so ein) Pech!	(what) bad luck!
perfekt	perfect
die Pflanze(-n)	plant
das Pflaster(-)	plaster
der Pirat(-en)	pirate
der Platz(-¨e)	square
die Polizei	police
der Polizei-kommissar(-e)	police inspector
die Polizeiwache(-n)	police station
Pommes frites [pl]	chips, French fries
das Porträt(-s)	portrait
die Postkarte(-n)	postcard
probieren	to try, to have a taste
die Prüfung(-en)	exam(ination)
der Pullover(-), der Pulli(-s)	sweater

R

sich rächen	to get your revenge
sich rasieren	to shave
rauchen	to smoke
rechts	(on the) right
regnen	to rain
reich	rich, wealthy
reichen	to be enough, to reach, to pass
reparieren	to repair
das Restaurant(-s)	restaurant
richtig	right, correct
die Richtung(-en)	direction
der Ring(-e)	ring
rostig	rusty
rot	red
der Rucksack(-¨)	rucksack
das Ruder(-)	oar
rudern	to row
ruhig	calm, quiet
die Ruine(-n)	ruin

S

sagen	to say
die Salbe(-n)	ointment
die Sammlung(-en)	collection
schaffen	to manage, to cope
der Schatz(-¨e)	treasure
Schätzchen	darling, dear
die Schatzsuche	treasure hunt
schau! schau mal!	look!
schauen	to look
scheinen*	to shine, to seem

schicken	to send	die Stadt(-¨e)	town
das Schiff(-e)	ship	stehen*	to stand, to be
das Schloss(-¨er)	castle, lock		(standing)
der Schlüssel(-)	key	stehlen*	to steal
schnappen	to catch, to nab	der Stein(-e)	stone, rock
(durch')schneiden*	to cut (through)	sterben*	to die
schnell	quick(ly), fast	stören	to disturb,
der Schnitzel(-)	bit, scrap		to get in the way
schon	already	stoßen* auf [+ acc]	to find (by chance)
schon gut	all right, OK	der Strand(-¨e)	beach
schön	beautiful, right, well, OK	die Straße(-n)	road, street
der Schuh(-e)	shoe	die Sturmzeit(-en)	stormy season
die Schule(-n)	school	stürzen	to fall, to plunge
die Schüssel(-n)	bowl	suchen	to look for
schwarz	black	der Supermarkt(-¨e)	supermarket
der Schwarzwald	the Black Forest	die Suppe(-n)	soup
die Schwester(-n)	sister		
schwierig	difficult	**T**	
das Schwimm-bad(-¨er)	swimming pool	die Tablette(-n)	tablet, pill
		der Tag(-e)	day
schwimmen*	to swim	das Tagebuch(-¨er)	diary
der See(-n)	lake	die Tante(-n)	aunt
sehen*	to see, to look at	tanzen	to dance
sehr	very (much), a lot	die Tasche(-n)	bag, pocket
Sehr geehrte(r)...	Dear... (formal)	die Taschenlampe(-n)	torch, flashlight
das Seil(-e)	rope	der Tee(-s)	(cup of) tea
sein†	to be	das Teil(-e)	part
seit [+ dat]	since	der Tempel(-)	temple
selten	rare(ly), seldom	teuer	expensive
setzen	to put (set down)	der Tisch(-e)	table
sich setzen	to sit down	toll	great
die Shorts [pl]	shorts	das Tor(-e)	gate
Sie	you (polite)	die Torte(-n)	gateau, cake
sie	she/it/they	tot	dead
sind	are	tragen*	to carry, to wear
singen*	to sing	treffen*	to meet
die Sitzung(-en)	meeting	die Treppe(-n)	(flight of) steps
so	like this	trinken*	to drink
sofort	right away	das T-Shirt(-s)	T-shirt
der Sohn(-¨e)	son	das Tuch(-¨er)	towel, cloth
sollen†	should, to be supposed to, to be meant to	tun†	to do
		der Tunnel(-)	tunnel
die Sonne(-n)	sun	die Tür(-en)	door
die Spalte(-n)	crack	der Turm(-¨e)	tower
spannend	exciting	der Typ(-en)	bloke, guy
Spaß machen	to be fun		
spät	late	**U**	
später	later	über [+ acc or dat]	over, across
der Speck	(bacon) fat, flab	überall	everywhere
der Speicher(-)	attic	die Überfahrt(-en)	(sea) crossing
die Speisekarte(-n)	menu	überhaupt	anyhow, at all
spielen	to play	übernachten	to stay the night
die Spielkarte(-n)	(playing) card	...Uhr	...o'clock
die Sportschuhe [pl]	trainers	die Uhr(-en)	clock
sprechen*	to speak, to talk	um [+ acc]	around
die Spur(-en)	trail, track		

um wie viel Uhr?	(at) what time?
um...zu	to, in order to
umsonst	(for) free
und	and
(un)glücklicherweise	(un)fortunately
unter [+ acc or dat]	under, among
der Untermieter(-)	lodger
untersuchen	to examine
der Urgroßvater(-ˋ)	great-grandfather

V

der Vater(-ˋ)	father
Vati	Dad(dy)
der Verbrecher(-)	criminal
verbringen	to spend (time)
verdecken	to cover, to hide
vergessen*	to forget
verhaftet sein	to be under arrest
verlassen	deserted, desert
verlieren*	to lose
das Vermögen(-)	fortune
verpacken	to wrap (up)
verschwinden*	to disappear
das Verschwinden	disapearance
das Versteck(-e)	hiding-place
verstecken	to hide (something)
sich verstecken	to hide (yourself)
verstehen*	to understand, to see
vertreiben*	to expel, to drive out
viel	many, much, a lot (of)
viele Grüße	best wishes, love from
vielen Dank	many thanks
vielleicht	perhaps, maybe
Viertel vor/nach eins	(a) quarter to/past one
der Vogel(-ˋ)	bird
vom	(short for von dem)
von [+ dat]	from, of, by
vor [+ acc or dat]	in front of, before, ago
vorher	before(hand)
vormittags	in the morning(s)
vor'schieben*	to push (something) in front

W

wachsen*	to grow
während [+ gen]	during
wahrscheinlich	probably
der Wald(-ˋer)	forest
die Wand(-ˋe)	wall (inside)
wann	when
warten	to wait
warum	why
was	what
was für?	what kind/sort of?
sich waschen*	to (have a) wash
der Weg(-e)	path, way, lane

wegen [+ gen or dat]	because of
das Weihnachten	Christmas
weil	because
weiß	white
weiter	further
weiter'machen	to carry on, to continue
welcher	which
wem gehört/ gehören...?	who does/do...belong to?, whose is/are...?
wenn	if, when, whenever
wer	who
werden†	to become
werfen*	to throw
das Werkzeug(-e)	tool
wessen	whose
wie	how
wie spät ist es?	what time is it?
wie viel(e)	how much (many)
wir	we
wirklich	really, real
wissen†	to know
der Witz(-e)	joke
wo	where, whereabouts
woher	where from, how
wohnen	to live
wollen†	to want

Z

zahlen	to pay
der Zauberer(-)	magician
der Zaun(-ˋe)	fence
zehn	ten
das Zeichen(-)	sign
zeigen	to show
die Zeit(-en)	time
die Zeitung(-en)	newspaper
das Zelt(-e)	tent
zerreißen*	to tear up
zerrissen	torn up
zerstören	to destroy
der Zettel(-)	note, piece of paper
die Ziege(-n)	goat
ziehen* [an + dat]	to pull, to give...a pull
ziemlich	fairly, quite
das Zimmer(-)	room
zu	too, closed, to, to X's
zu Hause	at home
zuerst	first of all, at first
zufällig	by chance
der Zug(-ˋe)	train
zu'machen	to close, to shut
zurück'gehen*	to go back
zurück'kommen*	to come back
der/die/das zweite	the second
zwischen [+ acc or dat]	between

Usborne Quicklinks

The internet is a great place to continue your language learning. At the Usborne Quicklinks Website, you will find over 30 links to carefully selected websites to help you improve your German. All you need is a computer with an internet connection - then just follow the simple instructions shown below.

Links for Easy German

To visit the recommended websites for this book, go to
www.usborne-quicklinks.com
and enter the keywords
easy german

You'll find links to a wide range of websites where you can:

• test yourself with online quizzes, drills and exercises

• listen to pronunciation guides

• use an instant verb conjugator

• look up topics in an online guide to grammar

• find out more about Germany

Downloadable puzzles

There's also a selection of Usborne German picture puzzles to download and print out. You can fill in the puzzles, then go back to the Usborne Quicklinks Website to check your answers. For each picture puzzle, there is a set of clues to help you.

Listening to languages

On many language websites, you can listen to native German speakers. This is a great way to improve your listening skills and pronunciation. Listen carefully, then repeat the words and sentences out loud. You'll feel much more confident next time you have to speak in class, or on a visit to Germany! If you see a loudspeaker symbol on a website make sure you have your speakers turned on so you can hear sound.

Net help

For help using the internet, see the Net Help area on the Usborne Quicklinks Website. There's advice on downloading small, free programs called "plug-ins", which enable your computer to display animations, and tips to help keep your computer safe from viruses.

Site availability

The links at Usborne Quicklinks are regularly reviewed and the websites are updated, but occasionally you may get a message that a site is unavailable. This may be temporary, so try again later, or even the next day.

If any of the recommended sites close down, we will, if possible, replace them with suitable alternatives, so you will always find an up-to-date list of sites at Usborne Quicklinks.

Internet safety

When using the internet, make sure you follow the internet safety guidelines displayed on the Usborne Quicklinks Website.

Please note

Usborne Publishing is not responsible and does not accept liability for the availability or content of any website other than its own, or for any exposure to harmful, offensive, or inaccurate material which may appear on the Web.

We strongly recommend that you keep your computer secure by using anti-virus software and by downloading the free updates for your computer software.

For more information, see the Net Help area on the Quicklinks Website. Usborne Publishing will have no liability for any damage or loss caused by viruses that may be downloaded as a result of browsing the websites it recommends.

Index

Acknowledgements

p.12 sunset, car/Digital Vision; **p.13** coastline/Digital Vision; **p.21** teenagers/Digital Vision; **p.25** Gail Mooner/CORBIS; **p.29** women shopping/Digital Vision; **p.33** Owen Franken/CORBIS; **p.37** girls chatting/CORBIS; **p.41** world map, beach scene/Digital Vision; **p.49** skiers/CORBIS; **p.57** Hulton-Deutsch Collection x2/CORBIS; **p.61** Owen Franken/CORBIS; **p.65** boys talking/Digital Vision; **p.69** Fotografica/CORBIS; **p.73** Neil Beer/CORBIS; **p.77** North American Scene/Digital Vision; **p.82** three children/Digital Vision; **p.83** Michael T. Sedan/CORBIS; **p.87** Joseph Sohm/CORBIS and astronaut/Digital Vision; **p.91** Jean-Pierre Lescourret/CORBIS and Michael Prince/CORBIS; **p.95** Stuart Westmorland/CORBIS; **p.124** man with headphones/Powerstock Zefa; **p.125** Kevin Fleming/CORBIS

First published in 2008 by Usborne Publishing Ltd,
83-85 Saffron Hill, London EC1N 8RT, England.
www.usborne.com
Copyright © 2008, 2001, 1992 Usborne Publishing Ltd.

Some of the material in this book was originally
published in *Learn German*.

Printed in Dubai.

The Doctor's Communication Handbook